To my husband Ed, in loving memory

Contents

Foreword

The annotated bibliography speaks so plainly for itself to anyone interested in The Rolling Stones that this introduction is
addressed only to those who might ask why such a bibliography
would be published. The first purpose is to serve those who are
interested in The Rolling Stones as a musical group. Second,
this is an experiment with a bibliographic style that deserves
attention because of the problems that were solved; the use of
title entry proved more advantageous than was expected at the
outset. Third, this is an example of how little control is meant in
complacent discussion of bibliographic control. Most of the
sources are difficult to find and are not indexed anywhere. At
what point in the future will the wrath of researchers descend
upon librarians if they are capable of providing access only to
material from commercial and readily available sources? The
history of knowledge demonstrates that the stone the builders
reject becomes the keystone of the arch. The analogy is not so
remote as it may seem in view of the course of modern music.
Rock musicians have played the mighty instruments of social
change. Long hair began with a musical group, The Beatles, and
possibly the androgynous image that fascinates the young has
its origin in The Rolling Stones. At least, as this bibliography reveals, some people think so. Finally, I am too close to librarianship as it is waged on the front lines to believe that any good

bibliography should be hidden from those who can use it. In my mind, bibliography is the key to librarianship, and there are always locks that need opening.

Jay E. Daily
Professor
Graduate School of Library and Information Sciences
University of Pittsburgh

Preface

The Rolling Stones are universally acknowledged to be a prime force in rock music, but they are more than that. Their lyrics, their personalities, their life-styles have affected the cultural milieu in general, especially the values and beliefs of the young of four continents. It is inevitable that when the social history of the sixties is written, they will be revealed as crucially important. Their role in the seventies is one that they will determine, but should they manage to survive assault from without, and their own excesses, it should be significant.

Central to any discussion of The Rolling Stones is the character of Mick Jagger, and he, more than any other individual in the group, has been subjected to public scrutiny in the past few years. His personality nevertheless remains an enigma to all but his closest associates. Strangely, despite the quantities of material that are available, the questions remain; his public statements do little to lessen the mystery.

This annotated bibliography is intended as a guide to sources about The Rolling Stones, featuring articles and books that are substantial and informative, but also citing those items that, though brief, provide insight or reveal hitherto unknown facets of the group. Since articles about The Rolling Stones tend to separate themselves naturally into time periods, a chronological approach seemed wise. Within each chronological grouping of articles and books, an alphabetical listing by title has been used. The reader will find that in a very real sense the history of the group can be read in the titles alone. An asterisk (*) before the entry number indicates items that are highly recommended. This sourcebook closes with a chronology of the milestones in the careers of The Rolling Stones.

Acknowledgments

Without the counsel and encouragement of my friend and advisor, Dr. Jay E. Daily, this bibliography would never have been finished, or perhaps even attempted. It was at Dr. Daily's suggestion that I used an arrangement by title, and it has proved to be eminently successful. Many articles were unsigned, and furthermore the titles were exceptionally intriguing in themselves; the title arrangement emphasizes this in an unusual and occasionally amusing way.

A word of appreciation is definitely in order for Mr. Charles Aston of Hillman Library, whose Special Collections area supplied so many of the alternative press items that were needed for this study.

This new edition of my earlier work has been completed with the assistance of two fellow Stones fans: Mr. Michael Colonna, filmmaker, who so often provided that spark of inspiration that archivists require, and Mr. Saul Davis, whose knowledge of The Rolling Stones is so much greater than my own.

THE ROLLING STONES

1962-1966:

A London Sound

When the Rolling Stones' first single was released in America, Beatlemania was at its height; in fact, the first five top singles were all Beatles hits, an unprecedented sign of success which has yet to be equalled. The Stones gave the Beatles the only competition they ever had, yet surpassed them only in the excitement of their performances, which became metaphysical events of the highest order. Comparisons between the Beatles and the Stones were fast and frequent in the early years and have continued into the seventies, a pattern altered finally by the breakup of the Beatles.

But the Stones were never imitators, and comparisons of the two groups must ultimately rest on sociopolitical and cultural influences. Unlike the Beatles, who were definitely the "Fab *Four*," the Stones were dominated by Jagger, and their music was more overtly sexual, more earthy and blues-oriented. Their sound, as created by the two Londoners, Mick Jagger and Keith Richard, was very different from the famous Liverpool sound that preceded them. The Beatles' tendency toward sweetness and nostalgia was noticeably absent in the brutally honest, harsh, Rolling Stones world view.

The early years were typified by the usual deprivation and struggles of a young musical group; later, in the first flush of success, the endless touring and the pressure to produce albums drained the Stones' energy and precipitated the near collapse of the band in 1967.

3

Jagger in the early years has been described as a "gutter boy" type; undoubtedly, in view of his upbringing and schooling, a self-styled role. Brian Jones was then the Sensual Stone; handsomer than Jagger, he was featured on record covers and in publicity photos, and he vied with Jagger for attention during performances. Many of the unisexual innovations later attributed to Jagger were first introduced by Jones. But as the writing team of Jagger and Richard gradually emerged, the musical influence of Jones waned. The leadership of the group was destined to pass from Jones to Jagger.

*1. *Our Own Story*. By The Rolling Stones, As We Told It to Pete Goodman. [New ed.] [Bantam Books, 1970.]

   Though written for youthful fans, this early book provides quantities of information about the Stones' childhoods and their early struggle for success. It was first printed in March 1965 and revised in April 1970 by the addition of an introduction briefly summarizing the events from 1965 to 1970.

2. "Air Pollution?" *Newsweek*. 66:76. Aug. 16, 1965.

   An example of "straight" 1965 reviews in which songs such as "Satisfaction" are treated with a kind of mock horror. There is no inkling yet of the vast social changes that will be catalyzed by such groups as The Rolling Stones.

3. "The Defiant Rolling Stones." *Hit Parader Yearbook 1967*. Derby, Conn., Charlton Publishing Co., 1967, pp. 21–22.

Interesting for its quotations by Brian Jones, expressing various aspects of his world view.

4. "The English Scene: Other Groups." *The Story of Rock.* By Carl Belz. New York, Oxford University Press, 1969, pp. 150–157.

    Recap of the Stones' history as the "No. 2" group. The relationship of the Stones to the Beatles is stressed and provides the framework of the discussion.

5. "The Pop Mainstream: The Rolling Stones." *The Pop Makers.* By Caroline Silver. New York, Scholastic Book Services, 1966, pp. 116–127.

    The Stones chapter in this "collector's item" is devoted mostly to discussing the nature of pop music as contrasted to jazz or classical music, but it does contain some worthwhile early photos of the group on- and off-stage, including a cover photo of the early Stones in performance.

6. "Pop's Bad Boys." *Newsweek.* 66:92. Nov. 29, 1965.

    Brief but insightful look at the Stones as they arrived for their 1965 American tour. They are contrasted to the Beatles, unfavorably, of course, in terms of charm and wholesomeness. Their music is reviewed rather favorably, however.

7. "Quick Take: The Rolling Stones 'Live' in New York." *Seventeen Interviews: Film Stars and Superstars.* By Edwin Miller. New York, Macmillan, [1970], pp. 234–236.

Brief 1966 interview centering on the Stones as stage performers, their reaction to female hysteria, to disc jockeys, to interviews in general.

8. *Rock and Other Four Letter Words.* By J. Marks. New York, Bantam Books, 1968. (10 unnumbered pages devoted to The Rolling Stones.)

This book of photographs and smatterings of text contains some exceptional pictures of the Stones, most of which were taken by Linda Eastman when she met them on board the yacht *Sea Panther* in 1966. Includes a bit of philosophy by M. Jagger.

9. "The Rolling Stones." *Rock From the Beginning.* By Nik Cohn. New York, Pocket Books, [1970], pp. 131–141.

Recapitulates the history of the Stones, especially their early years. Andrew Oldham's influence on the group, particularly his influence on Jagger, is emphasized. There are vivid descriptions of their early triumphs. The author concludes that their early potential was never fully realized, nor will it ever be. His ending is therefore sad, almost cruel, in assigning the group to oblivion.

10. "Rolling Stones: The Age of Innocence." *Hit Parader.* 30:8–10. July 1971. (Part one of Chronology.)

Half-serious, half-humorous chronology of the Stones, which interposes events in their career with world happenings, usually chosen for their ridiculous or ironic value. Useful to the researcher for its serious attempt to capture the important dates.

11. "Rolling Stones Story." *Hit Parader.* 30:13-18. Aug. 1971. (Part two of Chronology.)

    Continuation of above.

*12. "Shango Mick Arrives." *Goldstein's Greatest Hits: A Book About Rock 'n' Roll.* By Richard Goldstein. Englewood Cliffs, N.J., Prentice-Hall, [1970], pp. 27-32.

    Humorous and fascinating account of the arrival of the Stones in New York in 1966, during which visit they leased the yacht *Sea Panther* for a temporary residence as a result of their boycott by fourteen New York hotels.

13. *The Sound of the City: The Rise of Rock and Roll.* By Charlie Gillett. New York, Outerbridge and Dienstfrey, [1971], pp. 316–319, 326–329.

    The Stones are discussed, along with the Animals, as prime forces in English rock (other than the Beatles, of course). Their "stylistic" merits, such as Jagger's singing style, their musical influences, etc., are stressed.

1967-1968:

The Heavy Years

These years were troublesome and discouraging, typified by drug busts, reams of unfavorable publicity, and personal difficulties of various kinds, most of which revealed the Stones in less than sympathetic light. Amazingly, their music reflected not bitterness, but rather an unaccustomed tenderness and receptiveness. It was a moderately prolific period. *Flowers* in June 1967 was largely a collection of former hits and rejected tracks from earlier albums. *Their Satanic Majesties Request* was a trip that, drug-based or not, was like no other journey into space (inner and outer) produced previously. Reviews were mixed, however, and in succeeding albums the Stones returned to their blues roots, while continuing to explore the realms of human experience in more standard rock and roll formats.

The final album of this troubled period was *Beggars Banquet*, an unqualified success. Its outstanding cut, "Sympathy for the Devil," expressed perhaps more than just an indictment of the world's evils. It also expressed an image of Jagger that had begun to emerge — that of "Satan's Jester" or perhaps even Satan himself. Ridiculous though this seems, it invested him with an aura as "Prince of Darkness" that his protests of being only a musician were never able to diminish.

Touring ceased for the Stones during these years; for long periods they were prohibited from leaving England. Moreover, their emotional states mitigated against public performances, and the fact that the Beatles had stopped touring may have caused them to wonder if they could also retain popularity through recording alone.

Climaxing this period was their appearance in the Jean-Luc Godard film *One Plus One*, later released by the producers under the title *Sympathy for the Devil*. The film depicted the Stones in the process of creating the song in the recording studio and provided the first recorded glimpse of them at work. Other film ventures, such as their involvement in *Only Lovers Left Alive*, proved abortive, perhaps because only Jagger among the Stones was really interested in a film career.

*14. "The Age of Aquarius." By Geoffrey Cannon. *Partisan Review*. 36:282–287. 1969.

Framing with critical comment on *The Beatles* and *Beggars Banquet*, Cannon explores the difference in the Beatles' and Stones' political powers and concludes, "Mick Jagger is the Shaman of the emerging western world."

15. "Allen Klein: Playboy Interview." By Craig Vetter. *Playboy*. 18:102. Nov. 1971.

In an interview primarily concerned with Klein's management of the Beatles, one full page about the Stones is valuable both for its insight into their financial dealings and for its intimate view of Jagger at the time he was living with Marianne Faithfull.

16. "The Baddies." *Time*. 89:54. Apr. 28, 1967.

Typical of the reviews during this period, this account of the Stones' 1967 tour of Europe emphasizes the havoc of their performances, the rebelliousness of their life-style.

*17. "Beatles vs Stones." By Jack Kroll. *Newsweek.* 71:62–63. Jan. 1, 1968.

Comparative "rave" reviews of the Beatles' *Sgt. Pepper* and the Stones' *Their Satanic Majesties Request*, and finally the Beatles' *Magical Mystery Tour.* Intellectuals begin to take the groups seriously for the first time.

*18. "For a Rock Aesthetic." By Andrew Chester. *New Left Review.* 59:83–87. Jan.–Feb. 1970.

Contains perceptive comments on the Stones' political manifestations, as expressed in *Beggars Banquet*, in the context of an overall assessment of the state of pop music.

*19. "For a Rock Aesthetic — Comment." By Richard Merton. *New Left Review.* 59:88–96. Jan.–Feb. 1970.

Merton is keenly critical of Chester's article and includes an extremely lucid and sensitive review of *Beggars Banquet.*

20. "The Hair Come-on." By Trevor Millum. *New Society.* 14:100. July 17, 1969.

Acknowledgment of the Stones' importance in the intro-duction of long hair for men and of sexual ambivalence in the life-style of the young.

21. "The Hard Stuff." By Iain Stewart. *New Statesman.* 75: 216. Feb. 16, 1968.

A review of *Their Satanic Majesties Request* which contains some tantalizing comments on the nature of the Stones' appeal. They are seen as decadent, diabolic. There are suggestions of their influence on London society in the sixties.

22. "No Expectations No. 2." By John Kreidl. *The Age of Rock 2.* Edited by Jonathan Eisen. New York, Vintage Books, [1970], pp. 302–311.

Discussion of the Stones as culture heroes, including their political postures. Comments on the death of Brian Jones. Also brief discussion of the milieu from which the Stones emerged.

23. "Outlaw Blues." *Outlaw Blues.* By Paul Williams. New York, Dutton, 1969, pp. 19–25.

Review of *Their Satanic Majesties Request* by a noted rock critic and Stones fan.

*24. "The Respectable Stones." By Paul Barker. *New Society.* 10:6–8. July 6, 1967.

"The real meaning of the Rolling Stones trial is its frontier battle over privacy; it's a fight that recurs, and the time has come to redraw the line again." This is a legally oriented approach to the Jagger/Richard drug trial of 1967.

25. "Revolution . . . and the Rolling Stones." *Hit Parader.* 77:11–13. Dec. 1970.

Brief account of the Stones' appearance in Jean-Luc Godard's film, *Sympathy for the Devil.* Includes photographs of the Stones in a recording session, as they were depicted in the film.

*26. "Rock and Roll Circus." By David Dalton. *Rolling Stone.* Mar. 19, 1970, pp. 36–39.

Long, heavily illustrated account of the filming of the Stones' "Rock and Roll Circus" videotape, which was created in December 1968 as a BBC TV special, but was never shown. It is valuable chiefly as a historical document showing ·such superstars as John Lennon, Eric Clapton, Peter Townshend, and Brian Jones jamming together.

*27. "The Rolling Stones." *The Rolling Stone Record Review.* By the editors of *Rolling Stone.* New York, Pocket Books, [1971], pp. 88–110.

Includes excellent reviews of *Their Satanic Majesties Request, Beggars Banquet,* and later albums.

28. "Rolling Stones: Bad Vibrations." *Hit Parader.* 30:26–30. Sept. 1971. (Part three of Chronology.)

Continuation of entries 10 and 11.

*29. "The Rolling Stones: Beggars' Triumph." By Ellen Sander. *Saturday Review.* 52:48. Jan. 25, 1969.

Review of *Beggars Banquet* plus Ellen Sander's usual insightful comments about the current state of Stones affairs. Includes critical comparison with *The Beatles: Plain White Wrapper.*

*30. "The Rolling Stones' *Their Satanic Majesties Request:* An Exegesis." By Frank Kofsky. *The Rock Giants.* Edited by Pauline Rivelli and Robert Levin. New York, World, [1970], pp. 50–57.

Intellectual review of *Satanic Majesties.* Exhaustive; analyzes album track by track with many lyrical quotes.

*31. "A Sermon in Stones." By Charles Swann. *Twentieth Century.* 175:43–46. (No. 1033.) 1967.

"This is the year the Beatles abdicated as public figures, bequeathing their kingdom to the Rolling Stones, for whom it has been a very public year. Mobbed and manhandled in Germany, facing drug charges in this country (Britain), their image has consistently contrived to be controversial and anti-social. In fact, this image while successfully projecting them as performers, has also managed to mask their main virtue as innovators of a revolutionary approach to popular music." The emphasis on the Stones' lyrics in this article is excellent.

*32. "Stones." By Alan Beckett. *New Left Review.* 47:24–29. Jan.–Feb. 1968.

One of the first really serious articles to analyze the Stones' music in terms of the social and political connotations of its lyrics. Beckett covers the Stones from their beginnings to the album *Satanic Majesties.* A *must* article.

*33. "Stones — Comment." By Richard Merton. *New Left Review.* 47:29–31. Jan.–Feb. 1968.

Merton's article is based on the preceding one by Beckett and disagrees with him on several basic points regarding the nature of the Stones' eroticism and sexual role-playing.

*34. "Stones Piece." By Bobby Adams. *Crawdaddy.* 4:3, 44–45. No. 2. (This issue not dated.)

Excellent review of the Stones from the beginning in the Crawdaddy Club to the American tour of 1969. The account stops short of Altamont but includes many anecdotes of dubious authenticity (but great interest), as well as the author's own inimitable observations. There are photos of the Stones on the *Sea Panther*, plus the famous drag record cover for *Have You Seen Your Mother, Baby?* It contains the famous quote about Jagger: "Is it Satan as Christ sent to tempt us, or Christ as Satan sent to love us?"

*35. "What Motherfuckin Heavies." By Bobby Abrams. *The Age of Rock 2.* Edited by Jonathan Eisen. New York, Vintage Books, [1970], pp. 42–50.

A series of seemingly disconnected comments about the Stones, mainly tidbits from other sources, chosen for their provocativeness and shock value. Nevertheless, very amusing at times. Includes two memorable fan letters.

*36. "Who Breaks a Butterfly on a Wheel?" (Editorial.) *Times* (London). July 1, 1967, p. 11a.

The *Times* in this famous editorial defends two Rolling Stones, regardless of life-style, despite legalisms prohibiting comment. This was the turning point in their fight to escape imprisonment on purely technical charges.

37. "A World Turned Upside Down." By Geoffrey Cannon. *New Society*. 14:62. July 10, 1969.

   Dramatic account of the Hyde Park concert, the sequence of events, the implications for the audience, the effect of Brian Jones's death on the program and participants. Memorable quote: "Mick Jagger can make the world turn upside down."

The Film *Sympathy for the Devil*

*38. "Coming Together." By Joseph Morgenstern. *Newsweek*. 75:88. Mar. 30, 1970.

   Excellent review, one of the few in which the reviewer perceives the relationship of the Stones' segments to the whole. Surprisingly favorable for such a "straight" source as *Newsweek*, with such comments as "an audacious work of art," and, in regard to the Stones session, "a grand metaphor for all of us in our present spiritual apartness and technological togetherness."

*39. "Godard." By Penelope Gilliatt. *New Yorker*. 46:104–106. May 2, 1970.

   Very worthwhile review, concentrating mainly on Godard's philosophical intentions, but giving the Stones due credit in her introductory paragraph, in which she acknowledges their importance to the English social milieu of the sixties. Her comments on the song "Sympathy for the Devil" are certainly different: she describes it as "rather safe and short-cutting."

40. "It's a Put-on." By Charles E. Fager. *Christian Century.* 87:702–704. June 3, 1970.

   Not complimentary toward Godard or his film, this review rather surprisingly identifies the Stones as "giving some real interest to an otherwise worthless pile of footage."

41. *"Sympathy for the Devil."* By Stanley Kauffmann. *New Republic.* 162:19. June 6, 1970.

   Very perceptive review in which few value judgments are made, but in which Godard's political motivations and film technique are discussed. Little is said about the Stones except a comment on Jagger's sexual role-playing in a film that explores "the role of sex in revolution."

42. *"Sympathy for the Devil." Figures of Light.* By Stanley Kauffmann. New York, Harper & Row, 1971, pp. 264–266.

   Same as above.

43. "What Godard Hath Wrought." By Vincent Canby. *New York Times.* Mar. 29, 1970, II, p. 1.

   Very favorable review, concerned primarily with Godard's film-making achievements. The film is discussed in detail, as are the circumstances of its viewing and of its distribution. Very little is said about the Stones.

1969:

The American Tour

.

Feeling that their time of trial was over, the Stones began in 1969 to put their lives in order and prepare for a tour of the United States, which they now needed both financially and artistically. Unfortunately, though their goal was eventually accomplished, it was not without a terrible price. Brian Jones, beset by drug arrests compounded by psychological problems, was unable to tour again and, after clashing with Jagger and Richard over musical directions, quit the group. Shortly afterward, Jones was found dead in his swimming pool. The remaining Stones, with their new member Mick Taylor on stage, played a scheduled Hyde Park concert as a memorial for Brian and left for America under a storm of criticism for Jagger's assumed role in Brian's death, an allegation that had no basis in fact.

The American tour was a triumph that established the Stones as the "greatest rock 'n' roll band in the world." Begun with a trial run at Fort Collins, Colorado, it climaxed in a shower of rose petals at Madison Square Garden. Jagger had learned to incarnate the power of sex on stage with almost unbelievable force; almost as electrified as his instruments, he sent reviewers into spasms of description ranging from ecstacy to outrage.

The album *Let It Bleed*, released during the tour, proved to be eminently successful but tragically named, for another event was yet to be played — a promised free concert at Altamont, California, where the Stones were destined to experience a personal foretaste of Hell.

*44. "The Americanization of the Stones." By Ellen Sander. *Vogue*. 155:168–169. Feb. 1, 1970.

Sander produces yet another brilliant article on the Stones, centered on their Madison Square Garden appearance in 1969. She explores their significance to American audiences, reviews their performance at the Garden, includes many pertinent comments on Jagger. Article includes Cecil Beaton photograph of Mick.

45. "Free Rolling Stones: 'It's Going to Happen!' " By John Burks and Loraine Alterman. *Rolling Stone*. Dec. 27, 1969, pp. 1, 6.

Preliminary plans for a free concert are discussed, as well as the Stones' plans for other tours. New York press conference is mentioned, with liberal quotes from Mick Jagger.

*46. "Kiss Kiss Flutter Flutter Thank You Thank You." By Jerry Hopkins. *Rolling Stone*. Nov. 29, 1969, pp. 1, 6.

Coverage of the tour with vivid descriptions of concerts at the Los Angeles Forum and the Oakland Coliseum. Includes information about supporting acts and background about tour arrangements and production.

47. "Live-r Than You'll Ever Be." By Greil Marcus. *Rolling Stone*. Feb. 7, 1970, p. 36.

This bootleg album, according to this review, is the "ultimate Rolling Stones album," a fantastic claim the reviewer substantiates most impressively. Sample quote: "Jagger himself emerges as the most imaginative singer we have, if we didn't know it already."

*48. "On and On Mick's Orgy Rolls." *Freakshow.* By Albert Goldman. New York, Atheneum, 1971, pp. 148–153.

Excellent account of the Stones' performance in Los Angeles in November 1969 combines with rather ridiculous conception of Mick as *der Führer.* Contains famous comment on "Jagger jigging on the ruins of Western Civilization." After this bit of nonsense, Goldman concludes with an astute evaluation of recent Stones songs from *Beggars Banquet* and *Let It Bleed.*

49. "Peter Fonda Went Looking for America. The Stones Found It." By Jonathan Cott. *Rolling Stone.* Mar. 7, 1970, pp. 1, 6.

Describes sound-mixing session for *Ya-Ya's* album, conversation among Mick, Keith, and David Maysles concerning forthcoming film of American tour, notes on the Stones' plans to form an independent label.

50. "Rolling Again." By Hubert Saal. *Newsweek.* 74:137. Nov. 17, 1969.

Conversation with *Newsweek* staffer at beginning of tour. Includes description of *Let It Bleed* and a number of interesting quotes by Jagger and Richard on a variety of topics.

51. "The Rolling Stones." *Variety.* Dec. 3, 1969, p. 45.

Review of the Madison Square Garden concerts, with a vivid description of the Stones' performance and notes on warm-up acts.

*52. "The Rolling Stones." *Rock Folk.* By Michael Lydon. New York, Dial Press, 1971, pp. 137–200.

Long, immensely valuable account of the Stones' tour by a man who accompanied them. Outstanding in its description of performances; includes numerous anecdotes, personality sketches, conversations. *The* account of the tour, based on article in *Ramparts* the previous year. Many fine black-and-white photographs.

*53. "The Rolling Stones — At Play in the Apocalypse." By Michael Lydon. *Ramparts*. 8:28–53. Mar. 1970.

Nearly identical with previous entry, this article is profusely illustrated with color and black-and-white photographs, including cover photo of Jagger on stage. (These pictures are completely different from the ones used in *Rock Folk*.)

54. "Rose Petals and Revolution." *Time.* 94:90. Nov. 28, 1969.

A "straight" account of the Chicago International Amphitheatre performance with background notes on the Stones' most recent indiscretions and misdemeanors. A kind of horror prevails even in 1969 in publications such as *Time*.

55. "The Stones and the Gathering Madness." *Rolling Stone*. Nov. 29, 1969, p. 8.

Tour itinerary is announced after the tour is nearly over, *Let It Bleed* described, Stones' activities in Los Angeles discussed further.

56. "The Stones/Detroit." By Greil Marcus. *Rolling Stone*. Apr. 30, 1970, p. 58.

Favorable review of bootleg record due to its vitality and the crowd's frenzied response. Reviewer reports sound quality is inferior, but when played at full volume there is "something here that cannot be found anywhere else."

57. "The Stones Keep Rolling." By Ellen Sander. *Saturday Review.* 52:67–68. Nov. 29, 1969.

The Stones are depicted at a press conference and at a recording session. Their American tour is discussed in its various cultural and sociological ramifications. There are intriguing word portraits of Jagger's performances and off-stage behavior. There is also a cover portrait of Mick.

58. "The Stones Tour: 'Is That a Lot?' " By Jerry Hopkins. *Rolling Stone.* Nov. 15, 1969, pp. 1, 16–17.

Tour arrangements, descriptions of Stones' life-style in Los Angeles prior to start of tour. Photos included.

59. "Stones Tour Rolling On." *Creem.* 2:6. No. 7. (This issue is not dated.)

Report on the American tour with quotes by Jagger about America and the Stones' resumption of touring.

60. "Stones Will Play For Free." By John Carpenter. *Los Angeles Free Press.* Nov. 14, 1969, p. 35.

Interview with Keith Richard taped in Los Angeles prior to Stones' Colorado concert, which kicked off their 1969 tour. Covers all Stones' activities at that time including tour arrangements, Hyde Park concert, Circus TV show.

61. "They Put the Weight on Mick and He Carried It." By Greil Marcus. *Rolling Stone.* Dec. 13, 1969, p. 7.

    Discusses the difficulty the Stones had in 1969 in creating the crowd frenzy they had previously elicited so easily. Growing audience sophistication caused Mick to put forth Herculean efforts this time around, and though he succeeded it was not without initial difficulties.

1969:

Altamont

Conceived as "Woodstock West," the Altamont free concert was later to be known as the antithesis of that idyllic scene, perhaps unfairly since most of the violence was confined to the immediate stage area. But what occurred in those few hundred yards was indeed frightful and, sadly for the Stones, culminated in a murder within view of the stage while they were performing on it. Jagger's Satanic image could only be enhanced by the incident and it was, beyond even his worst enemies' expectations. Consequently, the Stones underwent (even for them) the most extreme vilification, and once more their stability as a group was threatened. The question of blame for the Altamont Festival probably never will be or can be assigned, but there is no denying that the presence of the Hell's Angels, the drug element of the rock culture, and the excitement of the Stones' performance all combined to create an incendiary situation.

The first cut of the album *Let It Bleed* was entitled "Gimme Shelter," and if the Stones were to be forgiven the Altamont disaster, perhaps it would be on the basis of this song, which expressed their own helplessness and terror in the face of the violence they sensed almost before it happened.

The events at Altamont were carefully chronicled on film by the Maysles brothers, who had been commissioned by the Stones to film their American tour. This footage was later combined with that shot at Madison Square Garden to produce a documentary film, *Gimme Shelter*, which may eventually be more important for its record of the Stones' performances than for its coverage of the nadir of rock culture at Altamont. This venture in "direct cinema" was released in the United States on December 6, 1970, the first anniversary of the Altamont concert, and was very favorably received by most critics. It also provided the "straight" world with its first look at Jagger, and the reviews of the film abound with florid descriptions of his stage performances. In fact, disbelieving critics literally compete with each other in expressing their horror, or fascination, or disbelief, or amazement, or whatever they find themselves experiencing as they glimpse "the other side" for the first time.

62. "Altamont, California, December 6, 1969." By George Paul Csicsery. *The Age of Rock 2.* Edited by Jonathan Eisen. New York, Vintage Books, [1970], pp. 145–148.

"Mick as Satan" account of Altamont. Slightly hysterical indictment of the Stones, Hell's Angels, and rock culture in general. Well-written nevertheless, with memorable word pictures of Jagger as diabolic prince.

63. "Altamont Death: Angel Not Guilty." *Rolling Stone.* Feb. 18, 1971, p. 14.

Describes end of the trial of Alan Passaro, the Hell's Angel accused in the death of Meredith Hunter, and Passaro's acquittal.

*64. *Altamont: Death of Innocence in the Woodstock Nation.* Edited by Jonathan Eisen. New York, Avon, 1970.

The book about the Altamont Festival, a compilation of articles and news reports, including eye-witness accounts. In addition, some excellent background articles on the Stones are combined with retrospective commentaries on the festival. Many illustrations. Although a number of the articles are critical of the Stones' role in compounding the violence inherent in the crowd, the book as a whole is not judgmental.

65. "Altamont Movie 'Before Christmas'." *Rolling Stone.* Nov. 26, 1970, p. 8.

Brief comments about the forthcoming film, *Gimme Shelter*. Also detailed report on lawsuits pending against the Stones and their promoters as result of the American tour. Gives revealing insights into their haphazard financial management on this tour.

66. "Altamont Part 2." By Michael Goodwin. *Creem.* 2:11–12, 30. No. 9. (This issue not dated.)

A long article with many eyewitness accounts of events at Altamont, including claims that Meredith Hunter *was* trying to shoot Jagger. No real blame is assigned; many explanations are suggested for the tragic events.

67. "The Altamont Trial." By Donovan Bess. *Rolling Stone.* Apr. 1, 1971, pp. 28–30.

In providing a detailed trial report, Bess necessarily recapitulates the events at the Altamont Festival, particularly those actions taken by the Hell's Angels. In freeing the alleged killer, the jury also indicated belief in the Angels' charge that Jagger's life had indeed been threatened.

*68. "Aquarius Wept." By Ralph J. Gleason. *Esquire.* 74:84–92. Aug. 1970.

Excellent and exhaustive account of the festival. The author is reluctant to assign specific blame, but is fully aware of the tragedy of the occasion and its implications for the rock world. Excellent illustrations of the Stones onstage during violent episodes.

69. "Calif. Rock Bash Leaves 4 Dead and 2 Born." By the staff of the *New York Daily News. The Age of Rock 2.* Edited by Jonathan Eisen. New York, Vintage Books, [1970], pp. 143–144.

Reprint of newspaper account of Altamont Festival the morning after. Typical of early reports.

70. "In the Aftermath of Altamont." By John Burks. *Rolling Stone.* Feb. 7, 1970, pp. 7–8.

Very detailed description of Meredith Hunter's murder as viewed from film clips; quotes by Keith Richard on Altamont, and by other involved persons — detectives, Hell's Angels, even Meredith Hunter's mother. Includes a number of photographs taken at Altamont.

71. *Left at the Post.* By Nicholas von Hoffman. Chicago, Quadrangle Books, 1970, pp. 150–154.

Typical "straight" press view of Altamont. Recapitulation of events by someone who was not there. Interesting for its viewpoint. Not specifically condemnatory, but rather disapproving overall.

*72. "Let It Bleed." By the editors of *Rolling Stone. Rolling Stone.* Jan. 21, 1970, pp. 18–38.

The exposition of the Altamont Festival in this special issue, almost entirely devoted to the event. Many pages of text and photos.

*73. *The Performing Self.* By Richard Poirer. New York, Oxford University Press, 1971, pp. 166–177.

Discussion of the reaction of the counterculture itself to the Altamont Festival, with particular attention to the special *Rolling Stone* issue, "Let It Bleed" (see previous entry). The author does not assign specific blame for the violence, but cites some cultural manifestations that were contributing factors.

74. "Perspectives: Altamont Revisited on Film." By Ralph Gleason. *Rolling Stone.* Apr. 1, 1971, p. 31.

More than just a review of *Gimme Shelter.* This rock critic examines the causes and the warning of Altamont for the rock nation. He declines to assign blame, but rather analyzes the forces generated by rock stars in their followers that have often brought them to the brink of violence.

75. "Rock's 'We Are One' Myth." By Craig McGregor. *New York Times.* May 9, 1971, II, p. 15.

Bitter attack on Jagger as part of general discussion on the collapse of the "Woodstock Myth." Blames Mick for Altamont violence and indulges in needless, cruel vituperation. (Article's credibility is at least partially destroyed by replying "Letter to the Editor," *New York Times,* June 6, 1971, II, p. 23.)

76. "The Stones Have Not Acted Honorably." By the editors of *Rolling Stone. Rolling Stone.* Apr. 30, 1970, pp. 1, 8.

Further recriminations about Altamont, focusing primarily on Sam Cutler, the Stones' former road manager.

77. "Stones: 'The Money is Superfluous to Them!'" *Rolling Stone.* Sept. 3, 1970, pp. 1, 6.

Discussion of the meaning of the film *Gimme Shelter*, including quotes by Jagger and by members of the Jefferson Airplane, who appeared in the film. The question of profit-making from the movie is a key point.

The Film *Gimme Shelter*

78. "Apocalypse at Altamont." By Richard Schickel. *Life.* 70:12. Jan. 29, 1971.

The reviewer's otherwise reasonable evaluation of *Gimme Shelter* is spoiled by a vicious personal attack on Mick Jagger.

79. "Apocalypse '69." By Jay Cocks. *Time.* 96:101. Dec. 14, 1970.

For its "straight" readers, *Time* recapitulates what Altamont was all about, concluding that the film is "strong, remorseless, but sensationalized." It also concedes that the filmmakers have given "brilliant shape and form to a nightmare." It is, nevertheless, not judgmental nor especially critical of Jagger, whom it calls "rock's definitive superstar."

*80. " 'Delicately Handled Dynamite!' . . . Or 'A Whitewash of Jagger'?" By Peter Schjeldahl and by Albert Goldman. *New York Times.* Jan. 3, 1971, II, p. 9.

Schjeldahl and Goldman present opposing opinions of the film and of Jagger in these twin reviews, probably the most thoughtful and important of all the film's reviews. Their comments on Jagger range from Schjeldahl's "a frail figure of desperate sanity," to Goldman's "the Prince of Darkness."

81. *"Gimme Shelter."* By Gary Arnold. *Washington Post.* Feb. 11, 1971, Section C, p. 1.

Arnold gives considerable background information on the Maysles brothers as filmmakers, discusses the film technically and ethically. His judgment on Jagger seems to be that inadvertently he released a lot of bad vibrations at Altamont that he was unable to control.

*82. *"Gimme Shelter."* By David Brudnoy. *National Review.* 23:381. Apr. 6, 1971.

Brief but honest, almost tough, in his evaluation of the film, this reviewer is complimentary of the movie's truthfulness and guts in depicting the reality of Altamont, as contrasted to the "gooey sentimentality" of *Woodstock.*

83. *"Gimme Shelter."* By John Carpenter. *Los Angeles Free Press.* Mar. 19, 1971, p. 31.

Rave review of the film is followed by an interview with David Maysles, who describes the circumstances of the filming and his personal reaction to the resulting film. Maysles also discusses Jagger in unusually favorable terms, describing him as "very sweet, loving."

*84. *"Gimme Shelter."* By Robert Hatch. *Nation.* 212:30. Jan. 4, 1971.

Particularly thoughtful review in which Hatch sees the film as documentary evidence of "a society at the end of its rope." His comments on Jagger's androgynous qualities are classic; his depiction of Mick performing onstage is one of the best.

85. *"Gimme Shelter."* By John Simon. *New Leader.* 54:19–20. Jan. 11, 1971.

Mixed review by John Simon, who admires the film's technical virtues but has an almost pathological loathing for Mick Jagger (see entry 449, his review of Jagger's film *Performance*). Nevertheless, his descriptions of Mick are undeniably amusing — not so his comments on rock music, which reveal profound ignorance.

86. *"Gimme Shelter."* *Observer* (London). Aug. 1, 1971, p. 24.

Mixed review that concludes film is "fascinating as a record of a truly terrifying phenomenon."

*87. *"Gimme Shelter."* *Pittsburgh Fair Witness.* Mar. 20, 1971, p. 11.

This unsigned review is unique in its viewpoint: that the film is, by its nature, sexist and indicative of the aura of male supremacy that supposedly pervades rock. The author uses Tina Turner's submissiveness and Mick Jagger's dominance as the catalytic forces that create the male chauvinist tone of the film. Though an unusual viewpoint, it is well written and reasonably presented.

88. *"Gimme Shelter."* *Times* (London). July 30, 1971, p. 6.

Favorable review by the *Times*, describing the film as "a powerful picture, not necessarily an altogether just or objective one," "intense, fascinating and genuinely alarming. . . ."

*89. *"Gimme Shelter:* Collapse of a Dream." By Arthur Schlesinger, Jr. *Vogue.* 157:86. Feb. 15, 1971.

Schlesinger regards the film as a worthwhile, if flawed work. He suggests that the filmmakers were reluctant to abandon the Woodstock myth and were too protective in delineating the role of the Stones.

90. *"Gimme Shelter*: Lesson or Preview?" By Tom Glover. *Circus.* 5:38–41. Feb. 1971.

Reports sequence of events in film, from the "insider's" point of view, for its rock-oriented readers. Unique for its color photographs of the Stones onstage at Altamont.

*91. "Jagger and Stones Make *Shelter* Film to Remember." By William Collins. *The Philadelphia Inquirer.* Feb. 14, 1971, II, p. 1.

One of the more sensitive reviews. In his descriptions the reviewer remains objective; his view of Mick's stage performance is humorous but perceptive. He is not judgmental of the Stones' role at the festival. His overall assessment: "Ninety minutes of film journalism that transmits as if by hot wire the electric frenzy of the world of rock at its own Armageddon."

92. "Jagger Sympathy." By W. J. McTaggart. *Forum* (Pittsburgh). Mar. 5, 1971, p. 11.

The writer presents an unusually sympathetic view of Jagger and the Stones at Altamont and states that the film is "a terrifying documentary which couldn't be missed."

93. "Making Murder Pay?" By Vincent Canby. *New York Times.* Dec. 13, 1970, II, p. 3.

Canby's second review reveals his afterthoughts regarding the motivations behind the film and the complicity of the Stones and their filmmakers in making further profit out of an event as tragic as Altamont. He questions the film's sensational and exploitative qualities.

94. "Of Sticks and Stones and Blood at Altamont." By Vincent Canby. *New York Times.* Dec. 7, 1970, p. 60.

The first Canby review, balanced and sensible in its evaluation of the film and the circumstances it describes.

*95. "The Rock Pile." By Henry S. Resnik. *Saturday Review.* 54:48–50. Jan. 30, 1971.

Gimme Shelter is reviewed as one of several films about the rock culture. Resnik has mixed feelings; on the one hand he criticizes the film for its amorality, regarding it as basically a "tribute" to the Stones, but on the other hand he praises the Maysles' technical brilliance: "'Their masterful editing has created the jarring and surprising impression of a headlong rush into satanic darkness."

96. "The Rock Tour That Courted Catastrophe." By Stanley Eichelbaum. *San Francisco Sunday Examiner & Chronicle.* Mar. 7, 1971, Section B, p. 4.

The film is recommended as a must for young people, although the reviewer admits it's a "shocker." The almost obligatory description of Mick onstage is particularly lively here. The reviewer's conclusions: "This is grim, high-powered drama strengthened by reality and marked by an element of riveting suspense."

*97. "Sympathy for the Devil." *Manchester Guardian*. Aug. 7, 1971, p. 20.

Very complimentary review, unusually sympathetic treatment of Jagger for an English newspaper. Memorable quote: "To lead the best hard rock band of his generation was never a matter of just being a singer and musician. He found himself leading millions and he couldn't do it without stumbling because he refused to compromise either himself or them."

*98. "*Wuthering Heights* and *Gimme Shelter*." By Michael Korda. *Glamour*. 65:59–60. Apr. 1971.

This nearly incredible comparison of two apparently dissimilar films is more noteworthy for its comments on Mick Jagger's personality than for its comments on either film. Korda sees Jagger and Heathcliff as similar figures — men of "demonic energies . . . capable of rousing terrible passions in other people without necessarily having to share them. . . . Jagger represents a kind of pure and undefined sexuality, not the sexual act itself but the idea and the power of sex as a force, unleashed, amplified, intensified by the pent-up excitement of his audiences."

1970-1972:

Entering the Seventies

The American tour and the Altamont Festival were followed by one of the Stones' frequent recuperative periods, which ended with their European tour in the autumn of 1970. Although some new material was included, this concert series was very similar to the American tour in content. Although reportedly not financially successful because of mismanagement, it served to reassert their supremacy on the continent, perhaps the most important function of any tour.

The album *Get Yer Ya-Ya's Out,* which was taped live at Madison Square Garden, was released in the winter of 1970 to critical raves and enthusiastic reception from record buyers. Business dealings occupied the Stones' energies for the next few months, and then in March 1971 they played a series of concerts in England billed as a "farewell tour." The Stones then changed their residence to the south of France, supposedly for tax reasons but also, they claimed, because they needed a change of climate and possibly a respite from the British authorities' repressive view of them.

In May 1971 the album *Sticky Fingers* was released, the first studio album in eighteen months, and the first album that would indicate the direction the group would take in the new decade. Reviews were generally very favorable — the old Stones magic was still there as they touched various bases in an obvious attempt to prove that they were what they were claimed to be, "the greatest rock 'n' roll band in the world." They included tracks of blues, country, and rock on the album, the first to be released under their new label, Rolling Stones Records.

In an unusual spirit of cooperation, various Stones began to "jam" with other groups so that just when their solidarity seemed most firm (for example, occupying the same villa at Antibes), the group seemed more in need of outside contact than ever before.

The album *Exile on Main Street*, the Stones first double album, was released in May 1972. In one of the most amazing turnarounds in rock history, the record was first received poorly by critics who called it dense, murky, impenetrable, but it was subsequently voted "best album of the year" in a number of rock magazine polls. *Exile*, admittedly a very heavy album not made any more appealing by its buried vocals, has proved to have enduring value not only for listeners but also for the band, which has used many of its songs onstage with great success.

Mick Jagger's marriage, in May 1971, was some kind of milestone, both for Mick and for the band, the ramifications of which are still evolving in his music and life-style. One thing is certain: the band's image has not been affected, and his fans are as loyal as ever. Mick made no film commitments during this period, preferring to be seen as the Stones' lead vocalist until the right script appeared at the right time.

*99. *Rolling Stones.* Edited by David Dalton. New York, Amsco Music Publishing Company, [1972].

The most valuable book on the band so far. The photographs alone are worth the price, and the text, by various authors, is uniformly worthwhile. The weakest section is that devoted to scores; this is understandable since, to do them justice, the songs would have had to be published separately. Includes a chronology that identifies highlights in the Stones' careers.

100. "The Americanization of the Rolling Stones." By Eric Van Lustbader. *Words & Music.* 2:16–25. Aug. 1972.

Discusses the Stones' need to understand and produce American black music and contrasts their early albums with those of the Beatles. Concludes that the Stones have indeed succeeded and, as the author states, "surfaced within the inner city of America."

101. "Rim Shot." *National Lampoon.* Oct. 1972, pp. 79–82.

Take-off on a "long-suppressed Stones album." Very funny pseudolyrics in unmistakable Stones style.

*102. "Rolling Stones." *Rock Encyclopedia.* By Lillian Roxon. New York, Grosset & Dunlap, [1971], pp. 422–427.

Erudite and yet humorous history of the Stones as a rock group. Perceptively written, includes discography. The author is an acknowledged expert in rock music.

*103. "The Rolling Stones: A Great Rock Group, Not a One Man Band." By James Lichtenberg. *Cue.* 40:8–10. Mar. 13, 1971.

One of the finest in-depth articles on the Stones ever written, with great insight into their musical and lyrical production. Many perceptive comments on the personality of Mick Jagger and his evolution as a performer. Analyses of Brian Jones's and Keith Richard's unique contributions.

104. "The Rolling Stones: Through the Past Darkly." By George Uhlman. *Rock.* July 3, 1972, pp. 13-15.

     Very comprehensive, valuable history of the Stones' musical development via an overview of their albums.

105. "We Can Piss Anywhere, Man." By R. Ballen. *Rock.* July 3, 1972, pp. 20-21.

     Primarily concerned with the Stones' image as expressed by their seeming nihilism, by Jagger's ambisexual innu- endoes, and by the group's apparent freedom to break society's laws of behavior and to release audiences from those restraints through its music.

The European Tours (1970-1971)

106. "Charisma Regained." By Michael Wale. *Times* (London). Mar. 12, 1971, p. 14.

     Review of the Stones' concert in Newcastle, England, the first to be held there in five years. Wale concludes his favorable and somewhat nostalgic report with the com- ment, "Mick Jagger is still the most exciting pop artist you can see live today."

*107. "Goodbye Great Britain: The Rolling Stones on Tour." By Robert Greenfield. *Rolling Stone.* Apr. 15, 1971, pp. 14-16.

     Humorous, anecdote-filled account of the Farewell to Britain tour in March 1971. Valuable for an eye-witness view of the life-style of the group, emphasizing the per- sonality of Mick Jagger, including his relationship with his wife-to-be, Bianca de Macias.

*108. "Mick Jagger Shoots Birds." By Sara Davidson. *Atlantic Monthly.* 227:96–101. May 1971.

Long and detailed account of the Stones' tour of Europe in 1970. Jagger appears as a distinct, not overly sympathetic character. There are many humorous episodes involving Jagger's behavior on and off the stage. The author is an admiring and kind critic, and the episodes have an air of authenticity. Important because of the excellent reporting and also the reputation of the magazine.

109. "Stones Finish European Tour." *Rolling Stone.* Oct. 29, 1970, p. 24.

Good account of European tour windup in France and Germany; stresses chaos and violence occurring during these last dates. Includes anecdote about Keith Richard's son asleep on the stage in Paris during that concert, fifteen feet from one of the Stones' giant amplifiers.

110. "Stones Plus Three on Road in Europe." By Jorgen Kristiansen. *Rolling Stone.* Oct. 1, 1970, p. 8.

Brief article about Stones' European tour, including cities visited, names of warm-up group members, account of their abortive press conference in Denmark.

The Album *Sticky Fingers*

*111. "Are the Stones Ready for the Seventies?" By Don Heckman. *New York Times.* May 2, 1971, II, p. 28.

In the context of reviewing the album *Sticky Fingers*, Heckman evaluates the Stones' awareness that change is in order if the group is to maintain its leadership in the seventies. The author concludes that "the verdict is still up for grabs," but that "they realize that ideas, images, and feelings appropriate to the sixties are going to have to change."

112. "Return of Satan's Jesters." *Time.* 97:60. May 17, 1971.

    Time, horrified as ever, reviews the album and reluctantly deems it impressive. It then launches into the controversy about drug lyrics being played over the air. The article questions the role of the Stones in the seventies, when rock has apparently taken on a quieter tone and so many of the big groups are dissolving.

113. "The Rolling Stones: A Promising Group." By Don Heckman. *Stereo Review.* 27:98. Aug. 1971.

    Heckman is very complimentary about the album and very optimistic regarding prospects for the Stones. He regards recent developments, such as the recording contract with Atlantic and Jagger's marriage, as signs that the Stones are straightening out their personal lives and preparing for a "rewarding career together."

114. "The Rolling Stones — Mouth, Tongue, Zipper, Stomach, Legs and Sticky Fingers." By Pat Patrick. *Crawdaddy.* 6:14–15. July 4, 1971.

    Favorable, track-by-track analysis of the album.

*115. "*Sticky Fingers.*" By Jon Landau. *Rolling Stone.* June 10, 1971, p. 42.

    Favorable, with reservations, track-by-track analysis.

*116. *"Sticky Fingers."* By Greil Marcus. *Creem.* 3:32–35. Oct. 1971.

Favorable, with reservations, track-by-track analysis. Includes many pertinent comments about the meaning and implications of the songs in terms of the current rock scene.

117. *"Sticky Fingers."* By Anne Marie Micklo. *Rock.* 2:26. June 7, 1971.

Rave review of the album with track-by-track comments.

118. *"Sticky Fingers."* By Rod Townley. *Jazz and Pop.* 10:48. July 1971.

Brief, incisive comments in a source hardly dedicated to rock.

The Album *Exile on Main Street*

119. *"Exile on Main Street."* By Lester Bangs. *Creem.* 4:58–60. Aug. 1972.

Very unfavorable review. For every good thing he has to say, the reviewer has ten bad things. Really dislikes this record. (Six months later he reverses himself and calls it "best Stones album ever.")

120. *"Exile on Main Street."* By Peter Knobler. *Crawdaddy.* Aug. 1972, p. 16.

Mixed review, primarily critical of the dense mix and loss of lyrics.

121. "Heavy, Heavy Roll the Stones." By Tom Zito. *Washington Post.* July 2, 1972, Book World, p. 11.

Unfavorable review in which the album is lambasted for being "repetitive, pretentious," and far too long for this type of music. The reviewer concludes that "it makes final the decline and fall of the Rolling Stones." He also dislikes the cover artwork and postcard inserts.

*122. "Mick and Keith Soften the Stones." By Don Heckman. *New York Times.* June 4, 1972, II, p. 24.

Very favorable review that cites "the softened intensity in what the Stones do and say in this album," and "an awareness that those who play the role of public symbols — totems, if you will — bear responsibilities." Heckman concludes: "The Stones are looking inward now, and if they help you to understand something about yourself, that just might be the most revolutionary action of all."

*123. "Stones Bounce Back from Exile in *Exile* Ode." By Robert Hilburn. *Los Angeles Times.* May 28, 1972, Calendar, pp. 1, 14–15.

Very favorable review that calls the album the most important since *Beggars Banquet.* Hilburn identifies its power as "the group's realization that the important part of its appeal no longer rests on its role as eyebrow raisers but with its ability to excite an audience . . . and that is their chief strength." Review includes track-by-track analysis.

124. "The Stones in L.A.: Main St. Exiles." By Robert Greenfield. *Rolling Stone.* April 27, 1972, pp. 1, 6.

Reports on Jagger's activities in Los Angeles during final mixing of *Exile.* Includes conversations with both Jagger and Richard about their new album and forthcoming tour.

125. "The Stones Tell Us What We're All About Again." By Jon Clemens. *Hackensack Record.* June 18, 1972, Section B, p. 23.

Very favorable review in which the Stones' identification with the United States is stressed. The reviewer states: "To every one of those million kids who will buy the new album, Jagger is the Exile on Main Street, the punk who made it. But, surprise, there are no Main Streets in France. I think he's talking about us again." In-depth analysis of the record follows overview of the Stones' career.

*126. " 'Tumbling Dice' Puts the Cherry on the First Side of *Main Street.*" By Lenny Kaye. *Rolling Stone.* July 6, 1972, pp. 54–55.

Mixed review in which the Stones are, as frequently happens, compared unfavorably with themselves. The reviewer states that "the magic high spots don't come as rapidly," and "they are at their most dense and impenetrable." However, he is encouraged that they are writing so prolifically and concludes that "the great Stones album of their mature period is yet to come." Includes detailed track-by-track analysis.

127. "What Hath Jagger Wrought?" By Patrick Salvo. *Circus.* 6:58–63. Mar. 1972.

Preview of *Exile on Main Street* prior to naming the record. Detailed account of its recording and brief history of the group for the latest rock generation. Also notes on the release of *Hot Rocks.* Many color photographs of band members.

1972:

The American Tour

More than a mere tour, this was a celebration and an artistic triumph, as well as a media event of major proportions. Riding with the Stones in their chartered airplane were rock critics, noted journalists and photographers, a novelist or two, and a number of "Beautiful People." All of this resulted in some books and articles of exceptional style and merit. In every city (no exceptions) reviewers were ecstatic — and vastly enamoured of the adjective. Describing Jagger, they literally vied with each other in creating superlatives.

There were many magic moments — the concerts at Madison Square Garden were, for the lucky ones with tickets, beyond all expectation. Those who were there will never forget Jagger's birthday party onstage and his encore with Stevie Wonder. Who would have imagined that Jagger would do "Satisfaction" for them? Whose birthday party was it anyway? If birthdays are a time for giving, that was a birthday indeed.

The film *Ladies and Gentlemen, The Rolling Stones* was subsequently created from concert footage, as a concert film rather than a filmed concert. Many reviewers thought that it succeeded; many thought that it didn't and that only the Stones live would be acceptable. In any case the cost of showing the film with its special quadraphonic sound system made profits slim, and the Stones were reluctant to compromise (as always) to permit its being shown with standard theater sound systems. Therefore the future of the film in mass distribution is uncertain.

43

Robert Frank's film *Cocksucker Blues,* also shot during the tour, is the property of The Rolling Stones, who refuse to release it, feeling somehow that it does not enhance their image. Their fans can only hope that someday it will be released, even for limited distribution.

Can the Stones top this tour? Their only competition is themselves, so that question remains unanswerable. But no sooner had the last notes died that night at the Garden, than the expectation started to grow again.

128. *Rolling Stones: Mick Jagger and His Tour.* Edited by Mark Pines. New York, Lyrical Image, Inc., [n.d.].

Special publication, compiled from a number of concerts. Includes notes on the tour's participants, an article on Mick's birthday party at the St. Regis, an excellent discography.

*129. *S.T.P.: A Journey Through America with The Rolling Stones.* By Robert Greenfield. New York, E. P. Dutton Co., Inc., 1974.

S.T.P. stands for Stones Touring Party, and the author records his impressions as he travels with the band for some time. Brief historical sidelights on the Stones are interspersed with apparently genuine experiences as the tour progresses. The book is straightforward, fascinating at times, a fine record of an extraordinary rock tour. Many illustrations, all taken during the tour.

*130. *Uptight with the Stones.* By Richard Elman. New York, Charles Scribner's Sons, [1973].

The author traveled with the Stones during their southern concerts and has provided a detailed and perceptive record. The book's chief weakness is Elman's remoteness from the Stones themselves, obvious and understandable. He observes them, but at a distance, and therefore can reveal little more than a simple account of their actions. The photographs, all taken during the tour, are outstanding and not available elsewhere.

131. "Aftermath." By Alfred G. Aronowitz. *New York Post.* July 28, 1972.

   Retrospective look at the tour, with special praise for Chip Monck's technical genius, Jagger's consummate crowd control, and The Rolling Stones — because "this music is a communion for people seeking an inspiration to escape from the evil in which it was bred, like flowers growing from filth, The Rolling Stones gave us that inspiration."

*132. "An Aging Kid Digs the Stones." By Peter Schjeldahl. *New York Times.* Aug. 6, 1972, II, p. 11.

   Schjeldahl concludes: "With less inventiveness, but with more genuine artistic instinct, they have created a legacy of these strange times that will stay crisp and authentic long after the Beatles' artsy-poo novelties have yellowed. I think it was in recognition of this fact, as much as in the general spirit of self-congratulation, that a lot of us at the Garden that night leaped, as they say, to our feet."

*133. "As Cynthia Sagittarius says — 'Feeling . . . I mean, isn't that what The Rolling Stones are all about?' " By Don Heckman. *New York Times Magazine.* July 16, 1972, pp. 10–11.

Excellent description of the Chicago concerts with special emphasis on the nature of Stones fans who follow the group from city to city. Valuable for its interviews with Jagger and Richard during their stay at the Playboy mansion. Concludes with the author's impressions of the changing Stones image, the reluctance of the group to write political songs, their tight security, and their enforced withdrawal from their fans. Illustrated with a number of tour photographs.

134. "A Day in the Life." By Tim Tyler. *Time. 99:49.* June 19, 1972.

Time issues a preliminary report on the tour as it reaches San Francisco. It follows the activities of a Stones fan before, during, and after the concert with total lack of comprehension and its typically Middle American air of shock and disbelief.

135. "Gotham Satyricon: Chocolate Mousse at the End of the Road." By Timothy Ferris. *Rolling Stone.* Aug. 31, 1972, pp. 22–23.

Mick Jagger's birthday party at the St. Regis is described in detail and illustrated with photos of guests. The final concerts at Madison Square Garden are touched upon briefly and illustrated with pictures of fans. The author states quite truthfully that by the time the group had reached New York, his publication had said it all. However, he adds: "When the Stones turned up their amps toward the end of each concert, what developed was less music than an exposition of the *aura* of music, a journey in the rarefied highlands of pure white sound and rhythm."

136. "Love Them or Loathe Them, the Stones Are THE Superstars." By Don Heckman. *Daily Mail* (London). July 20,
1972, pp. 16–17.

    British coverage of the tour in which it is admitted that
    the Stones are "Britain's biggest international stars."

*137. "Michael P. Jagger & Company." By Seth Goldschlager.
Newsweek. 100:54–56. Aug. 7, 1972.

    Fine overview of the tour touching all bases — the con-
    certs, the staging, quotes from Jagger, and the author's
    theories regarding the Stones' durable appeal: "The re-
    sponse this year confounded those who had thought the
    Stones' era over. The fifteen-year age range of Stones
    audiences — with hefty majorities of crowds under 18 —
    may instead have heralded a new rock scene: the Stones
    are now in a position to exploit the shortened life spans
    of distinct 'generations'."

*138. "Rock, Etc." By Ellen Willis. *The New Yorker.* 48:56–57.
Aug. 12, 1972.

    Retrospective view in which the author stresses not only
    the fine performances but also the Stones-consciousness
    that has enveloped the country, including the so-called
    Beautiful People, who were as desperate for tickets as
    Stones fans themselves.

139. "Rock Group Exercises Magic Unknown Since Era of
Beatles." By Jack Lloyd. *Philadelphia Inquirer.* June 20,
1972, p. 3.

    Explanation of the Stones' appeal for "those who are
    alien to the subculture that supports rock music."

*140. "Rolling Stones: Goodbye to All That." By Dick Lupoff. *Ramparts.* 11:12–15. Aug. 1972.

Account of the San Francisco concerts, the frustration involved in getting tickets, the pandemonium of the concert scene. The author philosophizes about the Stones and states rather provocatively: "Their attraction for audiences so far transcends 'mere' entertainment that it is tempting to suggest that they are not entertainers at all. Their importance is symbolic. They don't exist on a literal level." He speculates that this is their last tour. Concert photographs are excellent.

*141. "The Rolling Stones Go South." By Robert Greenfield. *Rolling Stone.* Aug. 3, 1972, pp. 24–29.

One of this newspaper's major tour articles; excellent photos by Annie Leibowitz; coverage includes the Chicago concerts and a number of the southern dates. The Stones' stay at the Playboy mansion is highlighted, as well as the presence of Truman Capote, Lee Radziwill, Terry Southern, and others. Many quotes from band members, touring crew, and guests.

*142. "The Rolling Stones' U.S. Tour: Riding the Lapping Tongue." By Terry Southern. *Saturday Review: The Arts.* 55:25–30. Aug. 12, 1972.

Very personal view of the tour by a respected novelist, marred only by his intense drive to be as "hip" as the Stones and their entourage — an impossibility. Nevertheless, he provides insight into life on a rock 'n' roll tour; he also probes Jagger's personality, the difference between his onstage and offstage behavior, and his considerable potential for acting. Illustrated with color photographs, including cover of Jagger.

*143. "The Stones." *The New Yorker.* 48:22–24. Aug. 5, 1972.

A retrospective view of the Garden concerts that concludes: "The Stones present a theatrical-musical performance that has no equal in our culture; . . . The group's musicianship is of a high order, but listening to Mick Jagger is not like listening to Jascha Heifetz. Mick Jagger is coming in on more circuits than Heifetz. He is dealing in total, undefined sensual experience of the most ecstatic sort. Wagner was interested in the idea of total art — total effect, total experience. The Stones are doing something similar. They have created something that is much closer to a complete experience than any other public entertainment available."

*144. "The Stones and the Triumph of Marsyas." By Robert Hughes. *Time.* 100:44–47. July 17, 1972.

This "Time Essay," an ambitious overview of the tour, states: "The point of the concert is not the sound but the presence of Mick Jagger, who is still arguably the supreme sexual object in modern Western culture." The article then quotes a parable and identifies Jagger as a modern Marsyas (a mythological satyr). It continues by citing the lyrics of "Memo from Turner" as the Stones' "presiding spirit" and then calls "Jumpin' Jack Flash" autobiographical! The color illustrations are excellent.

*145. "The Stones Blast Through the Land." By Thomas Thompson. *Life.* 73:30–36. July 14, 1972.

One of the most dramatic magazine reports because of its compelling color photography, including a cover photo of Jagger. (Interestingly, one of the few *Life* issues to be completely sold out.) The text is lively but superficial; nevertheless it is a *must* for collectors, and the author, visibly negative to Jagger, admits "he is possessed, as few performers are . . . with a stunning, electric-shock stage capacity."

146. "Stones Boom 16,000 Watts of Sound." By Robert Reinhold. *New York Times.* July 25, 1972, p. 23.

Detailed description of the Stones' sound equipment; really unique item for audio buffs.

147. "A Stones Fan Is . . ." By Henry Allen. *Washington Post.* July 5, 1972, Section B, p. 1.

Offbeat article about the nature of Stones fans, their evolution from screaming teenagers of Sinatra's day and their particular dedication and tenacity.

148. "The Stones: Long View from the Viscera." By Richard Nusser. *The Village Voice.* July 27, 1972, p. 34.

Retrospective look at the tour and the Stones' life-style. The author concludes: "The Stones are artists, first and foremost, and their work is the only thing we can legitimately criticize. Their private lives and how they spend their money are not our concern, unless they infringe on *our* lives."

149. "Stones: Rock with Power." By Sam Sutherland. *Billboard.* Aug. 5, 1972, p. 3.

Review of the Garden concerts that concludes: "Questions of mere technique are appropriate but inadequate in any response to the Rolling Stones, for the Stones are so much more than just music. They are, rather, a globally visible exercise in pure style. . . . As for Jagger, it would be pointless to rave: his presence whether it is evaluated as a symbolic cultural value or an extension of his music, is now so firmly imprinted on our minds as to be beyond description."

*150. "Stones Tour: Rock & Roll on the Road Again." By Robert Greenfield. *Rolling Stone*. July 6, 1972, pp. 1, 30.

Long, detailed coverage of the beginning of the tour — Vancouver, Seattle, San Francisco, Los Angeles. Photos by Annie Leibowitz. Cover photo of Jagger is singularly interesting.

151. "The World's Greatest Rock 'n' Roll Band." By Leroy Aarons. *Washington Post*. June 22, 1972, Section C, pp. 1, 15.

A reporter traveling with the Stones covers concerts in Long Beach, San Diego, Albuquerque, Denver. Valuable comments from such tour personalities as Jo Bergman (Jagger's "Girl Friday"), his tour physician, makeup man, and Jagger himself.

Pretour Reports

152. "Bless the Beasts & Children." By Patrick Carr. *Crawdaddy*. July 1972, pp. 25–28.

Preview of the 1972 American tour; the details of the staging are discussed, and there is even a drawing of

Chip Monck's complicated lighting arrangement. Cover photo of Jagger.

153. "5,000 Shout, Shove to Buy 'Rock' Tickets." By Robert Nolte. *Chicago Tribune.* May 21, 1972, p. 1.

Account of ticket sales in Chicago.

154. "Rolling Stones' Fans Beseige Spectrum, Stores." *Philadelphia Inquirer.* June 20, 1972, pp. 1, 3.

Account of ticket sales in Philadelphia.

155. "Rolling Stones' Jam in San Francisco: Ticket Computer Overloads." *San Francisco Chronicle.* May 16, 1972, p. 3.

Account of ticket sales in San Francisco.

156. "The Stones Before They Hit the Road." By Howard Bloom. *Circus.* 6:60–63. July 1972.

Brief description of the Stones gathering in Los Angeles before beginning the '72 American tour. Color portraits of the band members.

Concert Reviews ·

157. Vancouver — "The Stones Begin Their U.S. Tour." *San Francisco Chronicle.* June 5, 1972, p. 50.

158. Seattle — "Stones Stir Peaceful Seattle." By Robert Hilburn. *Los Angeles Times.* June 6, 1972, IV, p. 1.

159. San Francisco — "Getting Stoned at the Concerts." By John L. Wasserman. *San Francisco Chronicle.* June 18, 1972, *This World,* p. 25.

160. San Francisco — "The Rolling Stones: They Stand Alone." By John L. Wasserman. *San Francisco Chronicle.* June 9, 1972, p. 64.

     Exceptionally vivid description. On Jagger: "The arrogance of the man is extraordinary, the total control of his theatrics is awesome. Jagger is one of the experiences of our time, like him or not. There is a lot more involved than flinging oneself about." On Wyman: "Bill Wyman, who has not been seen to move since 1967, somehow managed to produce notes from his bass despite this handicap."

161. San Francisco — "2nd Honeymoon for Stones, S. F. Fans." By Robert Hilburn. *Los Angeles Times.* June 9, 1972, pp. 1, 14.

162. Los Angeles — "A Rolling Stone Gathers . . ." By Karin Winner. *Women's Wear Daily.* June 13, 1972, pp. 4–5.

     Review of Palladium concerts. Extended photo coverage of concertgoers and their assorted fashions.

163. Los Angeles — "Stones' 1972 Tour — Tighter Presentation." By Nat Freedland. *Billboard.* June 24, 1972, p. 18.

164. Los Angeles — "Stones Relying on Newer Material." By Robert Hilburn. *Los Angeles Times.* June 10, 1972, II, p. 3.

165. Long Beach — "Stones Reach Peak at Long Beach Arena." By Robert Hilburn. *Los Angeles Times.* June 12, 1972, IV, pp. 1, 19.

166. Chicago — "Frenzy for 5 Stones." By Marshall Rosenthal and Jack Hafferkamp. *Chicago Daily News.* June 20, 1972, pp. 25, 28.

167. Chicago — "Jumpin' Gas Flash Bops in Heartland." By Bobby Greenfield. *Rolling Stone.* July 20, 1972, p. 8.

168. Chicago — "Rolling Stones (5), Stevie Wonder." *Variety.* June 28, 1972, p. 51.

169. Chicago — "13,000 Mark Return of the Rolling Stones." By Lynn Van Matre. *Chicago Tribune.* June 21, 1972, II, p. 22.

170. Tuscaloosa — "In Sheer Excitement Stones Unequaled." By Scott Cain. *Atlanta Journal and Constitution.* July 2, 1972, Section B, p. 14.

171. Washington, D. C. — "Caution: Rolling Stones." By Tom Zito. *Washington Post.* July 2, 1972, Section C, p. 7.

172. Washington, D. C. — " 'Hello, Campers!' It's the Rolling Stones." By Michael Kernan. *Washington Post.* July 5, 1972, Section B, p. 11.

173. Washington, D. C. —"Still Dissatisfied, the Stones Are Back." By Len Cohen. *The Sunday Star.* July 2, 1972, Section D, p. 13.

174. Washington, D. C. — "Stones: Bringing It on Home." By Tom Zito, *Washington Post.* July 6, 1972, Section C, p. 15.

175. Washington, D. C. — "Stones Fans Gathering No Moss." By Michael Kernan. *Washington Post.* July 5, 1972, Section B, pp. 1, 11.

176. St. Louis — "Rolling Stones Gather Noise, Enthusiasm, but No Violence." By Connie Rosenbaum. *St. Louis Post Dispatch.* July 10, 1972, Section C, p. 3.

177. Detroit — "Mighty Mick the Jaggernaut Leads Rolling Stones to Conquest of Detroit." By Jack Batten. *Globe and Mail* (Toronto). July 15, 1972, p. 25.

178. Montreal — "Rolling Stones Equipment Truck Is Damaged by Montreal Bomb." *Globe and Star* (Toronto). July 18, 1972, p. 8.

179. Montreal — "Stones Fans Noisy but Peaceful." By Angela Ferrante and Victor Riding. *Montreal Star.* July 18, 1972, Section A, p. 1.

180. Boston — "All Ends Well — Despite Bust, Bomb." *Rolling Stone.* Aug. 17, 1972, p. 8.

    East Coast concert dates are covered, including the bombing of an equipment truck in Montreal, the Stones' bust in Warwick, R. I., for a brawl with police, and their delayed concert in Boston. One senses the exhaustion of the group as the tour nears its climax in New York.

181. Boston — "Newspapers Plan Suit Against Stones." *Washington Post.* July 20, 1972, Section C, p. 13.

    Further coverage of Stones' brawl with police in Warwick.

182. Boston — "R. I. Fuzz Gather 2 Rolling Stones." By Peter Brewer. *New York Post*. July 19, 1972, p. 5.

    Another account of the arrest in Warwick.

183. Philadelphia — "Columnist Came, Saw, Heard and Was Conquered." By Al Haas. *Philadelphia Inquirer*. July 22, 1972, p. 15.

184. Pittsburgh — "Rolling Stones Roll Up a Record." By Mike Kalina. *Pittsburgh Post-Gazette*. July 24 ,1972, p. 11.

185. New York — "Down at the Garden . . . Up in Central Park." *Daily News*. July 26, 1972, pp. 50–51.

    Photo-essay on Madison Square Garden concerts (centerfold).

186. New York — "Jagger and Stones Whip 20,000 Into Frenzy at Garden." By Grace Lichtenstein. *New York Times*. July 25, 1972, p. 1.

187. New York — "Jagger Steams and Stones Cook Along." By Don Heckman. *New York Times*. July 26, 1972, p. 21.

188. New York — "Mick Is Love to 20,000 at Stones' Bash." By Pat O'Hare. *Daily News*. July 25, 1972, p. 5.

189. New York — "Mick Jagger, 29, Gets a Put On, Turned On Sendoff." By Grace Lichtenstein. *New York Times*. July 28, 1972, p. 18.

190. New York — "Oh, the Dazzle of It All." By Patrick Carr. *The Village Voice*. July 27, 1972, p. 33.

191. New York — "Rolling Stones Rock Madison Square Garden in Finale of $4-Mil. U.S.-Canada Tour." By Fred Kirby. *Variety*. July 26, 1972, p. 47.

192. New York — "Satisfaction This Time." By Alfred G. Aronowitz. *New York Post*. July 26, 1972, p. 55.

193. New York — "Stoned." By Roy Hollingworth. *Melody Maker*. Aug. 12, 1972, p. 8.

194. New York — "Stoned Age." *Daily News*. July 25, 1972, pp. 34–35.

   Photo-essay on the first Madison Square Garden concert (centerfold).

195. New York — "Stones Are at Exciting Best in Finale." By Don Heckman. *New York Times*. July 27, 1972, p. 22.

   Includes coverage of Mick's birthday party.

196. New York — "Stones Bash — Nouveau Hip." By Jan Hodenfield. *New York Post*. July 27, 1972, pp. 1, 4.

   Coverage of Mick's birthday celebration at the Garden and the St. Regis. Includes photos of celebrities, custard-pie throwing.

197. New York — "Stones in Riotous Rollaway." By Robert Crane and John Murphy. *Daily News*. July 27, 1972, p. 5.

   Report of violence outside last Garden concert.

198. New York — "The Stones Jaggernaut." By Alfred G. Aronowitz. *New York Post*. July 25, 1972, p. 5.

The Film *Ladies and Gentlemen, The Rolling Stones*

199. "The Event That Wasn't, the Movie That Was." By Patrick Carr. *The Village Voice.* Apr. 18, 1974, p. 56.

Cancellation of the street fair is discussed, and an account is given of the premiere, "exotic beyond belief." The film is strongly recommended: "The best audio-visual work on the Stones to date." The reviewer sees it as "a super concert, not a movie about a concert or tour."

*200. "Grand Tour: *Ladies and Gentlemen, The Rolling Stones.*" By Jay Cocks. *Time.* 103:90. May 6, 1974.

Very favorable review in which the author concludes: "Whatever the Stones play at, they remain the definitive rock 'n' roll group, gutter-hard, brash and tough and tight. They are real monsters in the contemporary sense; outrageous, fine, unstoppable, uncatchable. Call them the best rock 'n' roll band in the world." The film is applauded for avoiding most cinema-verité clichés: "The music is all and it is plenty."

201. "*Ladies and Gentlemen, The Rolling Stones.*" By Vicki Hodgetts. *Rolling Stone,* May 9, 1974, p. 15.

Favorable review with an account of the planned street fair and opening in New York, plans for distribution, and detailed description of the film as a new concept in cinema, "a concert in and of itself." The author states that "it is the music that stars in the film."

*202. "*Ladies and Gentlemen, The Rolling Stones.*" *Variety.* Apr. 17, 1974, p. 16.

Exceptionally incisive review which examines not only the film but also the Stones' enduring relevance: "For some reason, sentiment eventually cloys, but tough, ascerbic cynicism has survival value." The reviewer rightly criticizes the filmmakers for their tendency to include too many close-ups and not enough full-frame Jagger. However, he incorrectly states that "only peak numbers" were recorded; the film is an exact duplicate of the Stones' standard concert format on the '72 tour.

203. "N. Y. Cancels Street Fair for Film of Rolling Stones . . ." *Variety.* Apr. 17, 1974, p. 4.

Full account of the plans for the street fair in New York and subsequent cancellation as a "public safety hazard."

204. "Reel Stones Concert: Glitter Headaches and Ziegfeld Follies." By Frank Rose. *Zoo World.* June 6, 1974, pp. 14–15.

Favorable review of the film, plus an inside look at the production and preparations for opening night in New York. The financial disaster of the street fair cancellation is discussed, as well as the mismanagement the film received from the beginning.

*205. "Rolling Stones on Screen." By Nora Sayre. *New York Times.* Apr. 18, 1974, p. 52.

Mixed review which criticizes the soundtrack and the "snubbing" of the audience by the camera crew, but praises Jagger as "just as exhilarating as ever." The reviewer concludes: "Spawned by the sixties, he now seems independent of any period, and even a clumsily assembled movie doesn't dilute his impact."

206. "Rolling Stones Street Fair Called Off After Court Orders It Moved to Park." By Deirdre Carmody. *New York Times.* Apr. 13, 1974, p. 19.

   Describes cancellation of the street fair scheduled for opening night in New York.

207. "A Stones Concert . . . Period." By Robert Hilburn. *Los Angeles Times.* Aug. 1, 1974, IV, p. 13.

   Mixed review, which contends that the film fails because it isn't able to generate the energy exchange that takes place in a live Stones concert. Hilburn feels that *Gimme Shelter* is still the most dramatic look at the Stones. He does praise the sound system and grants that there are some effective sequences.

208. "Stones' Film Preview: Hold the Pop Corn." By Ian Dove. *Rolling Stone.* May 23, 1974, p. 16.

   Account of the delayed opening of the film in New York and cancellation of the street fair, with plenty of details of "what might have been."

1973-1975:

Rock 'n' Roll Lives

Their triumphant American tour over, the band rested and then began to prepare for what they hoped would be an equally successful Far Eastern tour. They planned concerts in Hawaii, Japan, and Australia with much the same costuming and format as used in America. Unfortunately, their plans were frustrated when Jagger was refused permission to enter Japan because of a conviction for possession of marijuana in England. Japan had been a focal point of tour planning and it was a big record market as well, but the Japanese were firm and the Stones finally had to cancel.

During the Japanese squabble, a devastating earthquake struck Managua in Bianca's homeland of Nicaragua. Mick and Bianca went to Managua to find Bianca's mother and were shocked by the severity of the catastrophe. In the hope of aiding Nicaragua, and perhaps also of showing his better side to the Japanese, Mick decided to give a benefit concert for Nicaragua at the Inglewood Forum in Los Angeles. The concert was vastly successful and $350,000 was donated to earthquake relief. The very theatrical concert was perhaps a foretaste of things to come.

The Stones completed their dates in Hawaii and Australia and began planning for a fall tour of Europe. The album *Goats Head Soup* was now providing the band with the new material constantly needed for their performances. Reviews had been consistently favorable, and the Stones' perennial need to "go back to the roots" was much in evidence.

A hiatus followed during which rumors of Jagger's entrance into films abounded. But the Stones were really refueling for the release of another album and the biggest-ever world tour. In the fall of 1974 the album *It's Only Rock 'n' Roll* was released to very favorable reviews that frequently commented on the discernible change in the Stones' usual man/woman stance. It was suggested, and with some basis, that Jagger's marriage was becoming more influential in the creation of his lyrics. Since Jagger's lyrics have always been the story of his life, one cannot dismiss this theory without consideration.

When the Stones appeared on a flatbed truck outside the Fifth Avenue Hotel in New York and belted out "Brown Sugar" to a stunned crowd, the news was out, and the tickets were sold in a matter of hours. As only they could do it, The Rolling Stones informed us that they would tour the United States once more, maybe "the last time," maybe not.

*209. *Rock Dreams.* By Guy Peelaert and Nik Cohn. New York, Popular Library, 1973. (Eight unnumbered pages devoted to The Rolling Stones.)

Peelaert's paintings fascinated Jagger as they do just about everyone who has seen them.

*210. "Can't Get No Satisfaction." By Robert Christgau. *Creem.* 4:30–35. Jan. 1973.

Brilliant overall approach to the Stones in which the author plumbs their essence as it has evolved over the years. Discusses their apparent sexism, androgyny, etc.; concludes that in *Exile* "they are more into music and less into their own image," and that they are dedicated artists moving honestly toward their fans.

*211. "I Only Get My Rocks Off When I'm Dreaming." By Lester Bangs. *Creem.* 4:43–47. Jan. 1973.

A very personal article about what the Stones have meant to the author, illustrated by lyrics from their songs. Bangs recants his earlier devastating review of *Exile on Main Street* and now confesses that "it knocks me out of my chair." He also discusses the insularity of the Stones on their recent tour and the concentric circle of friends, tour members, media people, and fans that surround them in varying degrees of intimacy.

*212. "It Wasn't Only Rock 'n' Roll (and I Liked It)." By Paul Williams. *Crawdaddy.* Nov. 1974, pp. 46–53.

One of the finest articles on the Stones to appear in a popular rock publication. Paul Williams writes of his long association with the band through their records, assesses their impact on the rock generation of the last decade, hypothesizes that their best work is behind them but that "the generation who grew up with the Stones, who will eventually rule the country, etc., etc., will be shaped and guided by the music that touched them in their formative years." Many illustrations.

213. "Jag-arr of the Jungle!!!" By Patti Smith. *Creem.* 4:50–57. Jan. 1973.

Humorous personal view of the Stones; chief value is the amazingly insightful photographs that accompany it, many of which were taken during the years before Brian left the band.

214. "The Rolling Stones: Ecstasy and Evil." By Lester Bangs. *Rock Revolution*. Edited by Richard Robinson. New York, Curtis Books, [1973], pp. 38–46.

     This chapter on the Stones appears as part of the history of rock "from Elvis to Alice." It covers their general accomplishments through *Exile* and the 1972 American tour. It is perceptive and well written.

215. "Slaves of Rhythm." By Barbara Charone. *Crawdaddy*. July 1975, pp. 51–56.

     Conversations with Keith Richard and Ron Wood and vignette view of Jagger during recording sessions in Munich. Keith discusses their motivations for touring again and their musical directions. Ron Wood discusses the possibility of his replacing Mick Taylor. Jagger is pictured as he brushes off unwelcome admirers at the Munich Hilton. There are pertinent comments about various members of the Stones' entourage, their need for Jagger's attention in any form, and the frequency with which they are destroyed by "myth, example and expectation."

216. "Taylor & Jagger: Stories Behind the Split." By Vincent McGarry. *Rolling Stone*. Jan. 30, 1975, p. 11.

     Comments from both Jagger and Taylor regarding Taylor's decision to leave the Stones.

The Benefit Concert for Nicaragua

217. "Jagger Nearly Nude for Charity." By Jacoba Atlas and Howard Bloom. *Circus*. 7:64–67. Apr. 1973.

Brief account; many illustrations in color of the benefit concert.

218. "Mick Jagger, You're So Acclaimed." By Lew Irwin. *Zoo World.* Mar. 29, 1973, pp. 1, 10–11.

   Excellent description of the benefit with photographs. Also includes an interview with Jagger in which he discusses the concert, the forthcoming tour of Hawaii and Australia, his disappointment at being refused permission to enter Japan, and his future as a performer.

*219. "On Tour with the Stones." *Rock Superstars.* By Richard Robinson. New York, Pyramid Books, [1973], pp. 40–47.

   Lively, humorous account of the Nicaragua benefit, but more informative than many more seriously written pieces. Conveys a real feeling of having been there.

*220. "The Rolling Stones a Smash at Nicaragua Benefit." By Ben Fong-Torres. *Rolling Stone.* Feb. 15, 1973, pp. 14–15.

   Detailed report on the concert, including comments by Bill Graham about the arrangements. The fullest coverage of the event, with excellent photos of Mick performing on stage at the Forum.

221. "Rolling Stones Benefit Concert for Nicaragua." By Tony Scaduto. *Words & Music.* 3:72–75. Apr. 1973.

   Brief account of the concert; stunning color photographs.

222. "The Rolling Stones Rock for Charity." *Los Angeles Times.* Jan. 20, 1973, II, p. 8.

Review of the concert combined with information on Japan's refusal to allow Jagger entry into the country. Peter Rudge discusses the decision, which was based on Jagger's marijuana conviction in 1969.

223. "Stones in L. A." By Jerry Garvin. *Rock.* Feb. 26, 1973, pp. 16–17.

Detailed review of the concert with photos; cover photo of Jagger.

Hawaii Concert

*224. "The Rolling Stones in Paradise: Honolulu on $1700 a Day." By Ben Fong-Torres. *Rolling Stone.* Mar. 1, 1973, pp. 20–21.

Extended coverage of the Hawaiian concerts and the activities of the Stones in Honolulu. Excellent photographs by Annie Leibowitz. Cover photo shows Jagger sailing.

The European Tour (1973)

225. "Dark Horses on Parade." By Nick Kent. *Creem.* 5:28–33. Dec. 1973.

Intimate look at the Stones as they tour Britain, highlighted by conversations with Mick Taylor, Keith Richard. Cover photo of Jagger.

226. "The Rolling Stones — Down and Out in Europe." By Kathleen Stein. *Circus.* 8:24–27. Jan. 1974.

Account of the tour, emphasizing the frustrations encountered by the group: equipment difficulties, poor reviews, failure to get behind the Iron Curtain. Well illustrated.

227. "Stoned." By Michael Watts. *Melody Maker.* Sept. 15, 1973, p. 34.

"In a truly majestic show the Rolling Stones scorched back to Wembley. And they're greater than ever." Includes an account of Mick's hassle with Wembley's security guards and Marianne Faithfull's dramatic appearance in the audience.

*228. "Stones in Europe: A Hearty Welcome After 2 Long Years." By Paul Gambaccini. *Rolling Stone.* Oct. 11, 1973, p. 11.

The British tour is described, including the party at Blenheim Palace, the concerts at Wembley, and various incidents of violence by spectators and police.

229. "With Jagger in London." By Michael Wale. *Zoo World.* Nov. 8, 1973, pp. 10–11.

Conversation with Jagger on the eve of the British tour. Includes tour report, party at Blenheim Palace, comments by Jagger on the band's musical directions and the current pop music scene. Cover photo of Jagger's striptease at Nicaragua benefit.

The Album *Goats Head Soup*

230. "*Goats Head Soup.*" By Arthur Levy. *Zoo World.* Nov. 8, 1973, p. 26.

Very favorable track-by-track analysis. The reviewer regards the album as transitional, utilizing the strengths of *Sticky Fingers* and *Exile on Main Street* and avoiding their excesses.

*231. "*Goats Head Soup.*" By Bud Scoppa. *Rolling Stone.* Nov. 8, 1973, pp. 66–67.

Very favorable track-by-track analysis of the album, which is identified by the reviewer as "with *Mott* the best album of 1973," and "one of the year's richest musical experiences." Scoppa calls it "the antithesis of *Exile*," and "a romantic work with an unmistakable thread of life-affirming pragmatism running through it."

232. "Jagger's *Goats Head Soup* Jumps Back Into Music." By Steve Demorest. *Circus.* 8:64–67. Nov. 1973.

Combines a review of the album with comments by Jagger. The review is favorable, and there are many color photos of the band.

233. "Micky & The Poor Boys — Fourth Time Around." By Simon Firth. *Creem.* 5:26. Jan. 1974.

Favorable review from Britain. Firth discusses the Stones' incredible staying power and their meaning to various rock generations.

234. "Rolling Stones in Jamaica." *Rolling Stone.* Jan. 18, 1973, p. 8.

Description of the recording of *Goats Head Soup* in Jamaica. Notes on upcoming tour of Hawaii, Japan, Australia.

*235. "The Stones in the Soup." By Loraine Alterman. *New York Times*. Sept. 23, 1973, II, p. 36.

Favorable review with special praise for Jagger's vocals. The Stones' successful selling of their "bad boy" image is credited for their ability to attract young audiences.

The Album *It's Only Rock 'n' Roll*

*236. "But I Love It, Love It, Love It." By Jon Landau. *Rolling Stone*. Dec. 19, 1974, pp. 79–80.

Very favorable track-by-track analysis. The reviewer deems it "one of the most intriguing and mysterious, as well as the darkest of all Rolling Stones records. Time has become just one more reality to face and to deal with."

237. "*It's Only Rock 'n' Roll* — Can The Rolling Stones Satisfy You?" By Steve Gaines. *Circus*. 9:26–29. Nov. 1974.

Favorable review of the album with notes about its recording in Munich. Also discusses the effect of superstardom on the band, particularly Jagger. Many photographs from the Stones' second appearance on the Don Kirschner Rock Concert.

238. "Making the Stones' New Album." By Steve Turner. *Rolling Stone*. Dec. 5, 1974, p. 10.

Discussion with Keith Richard about the recording of *It's Only Rock 'n' Roll*. Keith also comments on recent books about Jagger, all unfavorably.

239. "The Rolling Stones: Ain't Too Proud to Rock 'n' Roll." By Arthur Levy. *Zoo World*. Dec. 19, 1974, p. 26.

   Very favorable review with in-depth discussion, track by track. The reviewer applauds the Stones' return to the roots once more in their abandonment of extra brass and backup vocals.

*240. "The Rolling Stones Now." By Ellen Willis. *The New Yorker*. 50:156–157. Dec. 16, 1974.

   Favorable review with more than usual insight into the possible motivations behind individual cuts. The reviewer delves into the implications that time inevitably presents to thirtyish rock stars. She also examines Mick's marriage in terms of its influence on the Stones' man/woman songs and concludes that "it just could be that Mick has finally met his match."

*241. "The Stones — More Mellow Than Macho." By Henry Edwards. *New York Times*. Nov. 17, 1974, II, p. 21.

   Favorable review in which the Stones are cast as trend setters once more, this time in perceiving that the pop music industry is in trouble and that *It's Only Rock 'n' Roll* indeed. The reviewer adds that Jagger's vocals are "the very definition of dramatic rock music vocalistics."

1975:

The Tour of the Americas

Having announced their Tour of the Americas in front of the Fifth Avenue Hotel while reporters waited inside for a press conference that didn't occur, the Stones arranged for ticket sales to be announced by radio simultaneously in all tour cities. In a matter of hours, all tickets had been sold and the scalpers went into action. But at least it spared fans the ordeal of spending days and nights on the street, which the devoted would have attempted.

There were changes in the announced itinerary. The South American dates were postponed for logistical reasons and because of Ron Wood's commitments to his group, The Faces. Later, three added dates extended the tour schedule by another week. It was the longest tour ever attempted in the United States, or anywhere else for that matter, and was intended to be the first of a series of massive tours of Europe, Asia, and Africa, as well as South America.

Reviews were mostly favorable, but the classic comparison was again in evidence. The Rolling Stones do not compete against other bands. They compete only against their younger selves. Just as the '72 tour was compared to the '69 tour, so the '75 tour was compared to the '72. One can easily anticipate the nature of reviews in '78 if the group waits that long to return. On the whole the '75 shows were longer and necessarily less intense — they were more of a frolic, they used more stage props, Jagger was more athletic than before, and the band played with a harder, raunchier sound than in previous tours.

Stones performances had become more professional, more polished, less spontaneous — this cannot be denied. On the other hand, Jagger had never sung better, danced better, or been more in command of the stage, and the band had never played better or more convincingly. Perhaps one change since 1969 did make a difference, although not necessarily a value difference. The younger Jagger performed with an unbelievable intensity — his moves were not so choreographed — one was not always sure that he would reach the microphone in time after one of his forays to the edge of the stage — but the fact remained that he performed as though possessed. In '75 he was still riveting; with or without a spotlight the eyes followed Jagger and only Jagger, but he was totally in command of himself in such a way that passion must be a little less, the precision paramount.

The well-represented "current rock generation" at the concerts meant that the Stones had once more gathered in the young. Having seen Jagger live even the younger fans were quick to assert that he was not too old. It was hard to imagine that this would be their last tour of the United States. Jagger's own integrity mitigated against it. If this had been a "farewell tour" he would have said so. But it was unlikely that the Stones wished to let another three years pass; as Mick so poignantly said, "Time Waits for No One."

242. "Back to a Shadow in the Night." By Jonathan Cott. *Rolling Stone.* Sept. 11, 1975, pp. 34–35.

Cott discusses what the Stones have meant to their fans and to society in general in recent years. He ends with a plea that they get back to basics, forget stage props and fancy costumes, and start producing new songs that are the equal of their old classics. Cott concludes by regretting that the band has, in his view, "gone the way of the ceremonial cult."

243. "Behind the Stones." By Mike McGrath. *Philadelphia Inquirer.* Aug. 10, 1975, *Today,* pp. 16–17.

Quote: "On the road and backstage with the most thoroughly professional — and most talented — rock group in the business. And with the Stones, it's all business." This is a fascinating hour-by-hour report on the preparations necessary to produce a show. It includes considerable technical information and concludes with an exciting account of the concert. Many fine photographs of Jagger, most of which are in color.

244. "Billy Preston's *It's My Pleasure* — Funk, Sweat & Synthesized Soul from the Stones' Pianoman." By Mitchell Glazer. *Circus Raves.* 2:61–66. Sept. 1975.

Although the text is a review of Preston's work in general and his new album in particular, the photographs, numerous and in color, are some of the finest of the Stones in action in '75.

*245. "Can the Stones Still Cut It? A Close-up Personal Report on the Men in the Band." By Karen Durbin. *The Village Voice.* June 23, 1975, pp. 6–9.

Brilliant article by a reporter who traveled with the band for several days, from Baton Rouge to Kansas City. She records much backstage activity and her attempt to interview Jagger. The latter must be deemed a mixed success resulting from interruptions and Jagger's macho sense of humor. Her impressions of band members are sensitive and apparently reliable. Fine illustrations complement the first-rate text.

*246. "Hip Vaudeville: On Tour with Mick the Tease and His Rolling Stones." By Frank Conroy. *New York Times Magazine.* June 22, 1975, pp. 26–31.

Very important article that covers preparations for the concert tour, which took place at Montauk, rehearsals in the hangar at Stewart Airport, and the first date at Baton Rouge. Invaluable for its look at the Stones pretour lifestyle and for its analysis of their performing art. The author's description of Mick's "Come and Get Me" dance is classic. Conroy concludes that Jagger's artistry lies in his consummate ability to tease his audience so that "men, women and children . . . eventually reach the point where they want to climb up there and eat him alive."

247. "I Call and Call and Call on Mick." By Dave Marsh. *Rolling Stone.* Sept. 11, 1975, pp. 31–33.

Describes the author's attempts over a period of several days, to complete a promised interview with Mick. Also provides a glimpse of the Stones' after-hours activities in Los Angeles and San Francisco.

*248. "It Isn't Only Rock and Roll." By Robert Christgau. *The Village Voice.* June 30, 1975, p. 115.

Quote: "The Stones are transcendent when they're good and merely good when they're bad." The author reviews the Toronto and New York concerts and compares the '72 and '75 shows. He feels that the Stones have peaked, but admits that his friends think the current shows are the best they've ever seen. He concludes: "I wonder what I'll think of them in 1978."

*249. "L. A. Friday Night." By Jann Wenner. *Rolling Stone.* Sept. 11, 1975, pp. 36–38.

More concerned with the style of the whole tour than just reviewing the Forum shows, Wenner's comments are generally very favorable. He disusses Keith's importance to the band, the differences in the sound without a brass section, Billy Preston's contributions, and Jagger's unique talents. Of the latter, Wenner states, in regard to Mick's water dousing of himself and his audience, "It is a gesture designed to self-deprecate and thus endear the audience to a showman of the highest, rarest order." He concludes: "They are better as a band in 1975 than at any previous time." The article includes excellent illustrations and cover photo of Mick.

*250. "Memphis Hosts Stones; Honky-Tonk Time; Arkansas Busts Richard; Rinky-Dink Crime." By Robert Palmer. *Rolling Stone.* Aug. 14, 1975, pp. 9, 12–13.

Detailed coverage of the Memphis gig, including the Stones' arrival at the Hilton Inn, the inclusion of Furry Lewis as an opening act, the show itself, and a brief interview with Charlie Watts. Concludes with Keith's arrest in Fordyce, Arkansas, for carrying a "concealed weapon" — a hunting knife. Many illustrations before and during concert.

251. "My Secret Life with the Rolling Stones." By Joyce Maynard. *New York Times.* June 22, 1975, II, pp. 1, 23.

Highly personal view of the Stones by a fan who records her changing reactions to the group as she matures. She concludes that perhaps the times are no longer suited to rock music and confides that she now likes to waltz.

*252. "No One Could Invent Mick Jagger." By Joyce Maynard. *New York Times.* June 29, 1975, II, p. 17.

The author explores Mick's childlike qualities as perceived by her at the Boston Garden Concert. These are identified in his looseness and artlessness on stage and his freedom of movement and action. She also perceives the singular appropriateness of his name. Her analysis of the Stones' sexual humor is very insightful — very few writers have stated that "they laugh at living and make us do the same." She claims that this is true of the current tour, if not always of the past. A special, uniquely worthwhile article.

*253. "On the Road with the Rolling Stones." By John Rockwell. *New York Times.* June 9, 1975, p. 44.

Report from Kansas City and San Antonio that deals primarily with the logistical planning necessary to keep the Stones' gigantic tour machine running. There are quotes from tour manager Peter Rudge and vignette glimpses of the Stones as they work and try to relax. The author states: "The Stones are musicians; they think and feel music all the time, and all the passing excitements and boredom of life on the road revolve ultimately around music."

*254. "Rocky Road: Frenetic Manager Rolls Rolling Stones Along on a Tautly Run Tour." By Michael J. Connor. *Wall Street Journal.* June 20, 1975, pp. 1, 23.

Major article in an unlikely source; it emphasizes, as might be expected, the financial arrangements necessary for a tour of this size. Tour manager Peter Rudge is interviewed about the details of his operation. His comments are pungent and range from serious to very amusing.

255. "The Rolling Stones." *Rock Superstars Poster Magazine.* (Special Issue.) 1975. [n.p.].

Another tribute to the '75 tour: text reviewing history of the Stones, many photos, all in color, mainly from current tour. Also poster of Jagger.

*256. "The Rolling Stones—A Celebration." Text by Nik Cohn. *Circus.* (Pinups No. 2 — Special Issue.) 1975. 71 pp.

This is a feast of photographs, most of which had not appeared previously. Some are from Cecil Beaton's gallery of photographs of Jagger. The text recapitulates the Stones' whole career and is necessarily rather superficial, though well written. In his conclusion the author, who has always shown ambivalence about the group's future, acknowledges its lasting importance: "In fifty years, I have no doubt, it will be Jagger and the Stones, rather than the Beatles or Bob Dylan, that historians will choose to epitomize the pop age. . . . it has been the Stones, more than anyone, who have expressed their time, who have summed up everything good and everything bad about Rock."

*257. "Rolling Stones Still Personify Rock As They Begin Tour of U.S. in South." By John Rockwell. *New York Times.* June 3, 1975, p. 25.

The *Times's* first concert review dispels any notions that "the Stones have settled into burnt-out imitations of themselves." Instead, it reaffirms that "the Stones are unquestionably the best performing rock band in the world and . . . the most important, influential figures in rock." The Baton Rouge concerts are described in detail, and Rockwell stresses that "the Stones clearly want to be thought of as an ongoing working band, and not as custodians of nostalgia."

*258. "The Rolling Stones: Their 1975 Tour. World's Greatest Performing Band Bewilders the South; Baptized in Baton Rouge; Castrated in San Antone." Observed by Chet Flippo. Photographed by Annie Leibowitz. *Rolling Stone.* July 17, 1975, pp. 32–37, 62–64.

An article of major importance and this publication's most intense coverage. It begins in Montauk with rehearsal activity and follows the band through its first two dates. There are brief interviews with band members and a fairly lengthy talk with Jagger about the tour and about his future plans. The photography is superb, and the cover portrait of Jagger and Richard is unforgettable.

259. "Stones Come Out of the Closet." By Lisa Robinson. *Creem.* 7:57–59. Sept. 1975.

The Stones' press representative writes about the various outfits worn by the Stones onstage, emphasizing Jagger's many costumes. Contains a number of amusing anecdotes and fine photographs.

*260. "The Stones Roll On: A Scare in Boston; Success in Toronto; A Slip in New York." By Dave Marsh. *Rolling Stone.* July 31, 1975, pp. 9–10, 18.

In-depth coverage of the tour, with many anecdotes and photos; emphasis is on New York, where, according to Marsh, concerts were below expectations. The first three nights at Madison Square Garden are described in detail —opening night, particularly its weaknesses, is stressed, although it is admitted that "Tuesday was inspired."

261. "Stones' U. S. Tour to Gross $13-Mil." *Variety.* Aug. 6, 1975, p. 45.

    Windup article announces additional tour dates in Louisville, Hampton Roads, and Buffalo and postponement of South American dates, for logistical reasons, until January. Also mentions the delay in The Faces' tour to accommodate Ron Wood and allow him to complete his commitments to the Stones.

262. "Swooping Over America with the Stones." By Stephen Demorest. *Circus.* 9:50–53. Sept. 1975.

    Excellent overview of the entire tour including technical information, vignette views of the various band members, numerous anecdotes, many fine black-and-white photographs. This issue also contains posters of Mick and Keith.

*263. "Sympathy for the Stones." By Ellen Willis. *The New Yorker.* 51:72–74. July 14, 1975.

    The author, an admitted Stones fan as well as a noted rock critic, reports on the New York concerts, pointing out significant differences among them. She concludes that this time Jagger "whose preeminence depends on his erotic power," has chosen "to play down his sexuality onstage." Instead, "Jumpin' Jack Flash is an imp, not a man — a lightning rod for an impersonal, asexual, super-human energy." Willis's description of Thursday night's violence, when a cherry bomb exploded near the stage, is dramatic, and her conclusion is interesting: "The challenge of a difficult, capricious audience had forced Jagger to be harder, more serious, more real."

Pretour Reports

264. " 'Anti-Scalper' Ticket Plan Praised." By Robert Hilburn. *Los Angeles Times.* May 3, 1975, II, p. 8.

    Account of ticket sales in Los Angeles and an analysis of the Stones' approach to a problem that had resulted in inconvenience and even injury to buyers in the past. Hilburn reports that most rock fans seem pleased by a method that discourages "camping out" for days in front of ticket windows.

265. "Jagger Cuts Hand." *Variety.* May 21, 1975, p. 61.

    Describes the circumstances of Mick's accident in Montauk before the start of the tour.

266. "Mick and the Stones Roll Out Their Act in Rainy New York." *People.* 3:16. May 19, 1975.

    The impromptu concert on Fifth Avenue is highlighted in this tour announcement. Photographs of Jagger performing on a flatbed truck are excellent.

267. "New Stones Tour to Add Old Face." By Steve Weitzman. *Rolling Stone.* June 5, 1975, p. 14.

    In a brief interview Jagger discusses the addition of Ron Wood for this tour.

268. "The Obsolescence of God's Own Punks." By Nik Cohn. *New York.* 8:72–74. June 2, 1975.

It is impossible to forget that this writer assigned The Rolling Stones to oblivion as far back as 1970 (see entry 9). Yet Cohn has always indicated great admiration for the group and keen awareness of the basis for its appeal. Here he accuses the Stones of "self-parody" and says of Jagger that "even in decline, he carried a surface dazzle which passed for excitement," admitting that "physically, of course, he was beautiful to watch." Cohn's article, sandwiched between two of the most successful concert tours ever to take place, is inexplicable.

269. "The Pragmatic Jagger: Planning Stones' Onslaught." By John Rockwell. *New York Times.* May 15, 1975, p. 50.

Mick is interviewed at LaGuardia Airport about tour plans — staging, costumes, songs. Mick discounts speculation that this may be the group's last tour and comments briefly on his future as an entertainer.

270. "The Rolling Stones' New Face." By Ron Ross. *Phonograph Record Magazine.* 5:18. June 1975.

Discusses the addition of Ron Wood to the group and his value; he is "a reflection of the '70s" and has the "ability to fit into a group context without sacrificing any of his individualism." The author also cites Jagger's continuing importance as an "athletic sex symbol that still inspires 15 year old girls to grow up faster than boys do, though Mick's twice their age." Concludes with a discussion of forthcoming albums both from the Stones and from Allen Klein's ABKCO.

271. "The Rolling Stones on Tour." By Jacqueline Trescott. *Washington Post.* May 2, 1975, Section B, p. 1.

Detailed report of the Fifth Avenue concert and brief overview of forthcoming tour plans. Crowd reaction to ten-minute concert is stressed.

272. "Rolling Stones: Tour of the Americas 75." *Rolling Stone.* June 5, 1975, p. 23.

Original tour itinerary, which was later expanded to include three more U. S. dates, while the South American segment was postponed.

273. "Scrappers' Scrapbook." *Circus.* 9:37–44. Aug. 1975.

A collection of classic Stones photographs, many in color, from the beginning of their career. Pretour interest is heightened by the inclusion of the rejected *Beggars Banquet* cover and a number of color shots from "Rock and Roll Circus." Includes discography.

274. "Stones Loom, Tickets Boom." *Rolling Stone.* June 19, 1975, p. 15.

In addition to giving an account of instant ticket sellouts, the author describes Mick's injuries to his hand and arm in Montauk. The Stones deny that this is their last tour, but Jagger says, "I'd rather be dead than sing 'Satisfaction' when I'm 45."

*275. "The Stones Movie You'll Never See." By Greil Marcus. *The Village Voice.* June 9, 1975, p. 126.

Pretour interest includes the status of the famous underground film of the '72 tour, Robert Frank's *Cocksucker*

Blues. Marcus reveals that Jagger refuses to allow the film to be shown. Marcus believes that "it does not celebrate the Stones, nor show that they are the greatest rock and roll band in the world." It is also clear that the film as edited by Frank would have difficulty achieving a rating that would enable a young audience to view it.

276. "Stones Take Off on Mammoth Tours." *Gig.* 2:19. Aug. 1975.

    Brief coverage of forthcoming tour plans and albums *Metamorphosis* and *Made in the Shade.* Cover photo of

277. "Stones Tour Is On and So Is Ticket Rush." By John Rockwell. *New York Times.* May 2, 1975, p. 19.

    The Stones' ten-minute performance outside the Fifth Avenue Hotel is reported, as well as the general announcement of concert locations and almost instantaneous ticket sellout. Peter Rudge is interviewed on the ticket system and the Stones' attempt to make it equitable and painless for purchasers.

Concert Reviews

278. San Antonio — "Rolling Stones Tour Hits a Snag." By Robert Hilburn. *Los Angeles Times.* June 7, 1975, II, p. 5.

    Review of the San Antonio concert with emphasis on the Stones' troubles with police authorities over their inflatable phallus and their subsequent decision to cancel its appearance rather than provoke legal action. Also includes an interview with Keith about the song selections and a talk with Mick about the group's future plans. Jagger.

279. Milwaukee — "Rolling Stones Cracking B. O. Records in Nationwide Tour." *Variety.* June 11, 1975, p. 59.

280. Milwaukee — "Stones' Big Rival — Their Past." By Damien Jaques. *Milwaukee Journal.* June 9, 1975, Pt. 2, p. 1.

281. Milwaukee — "Stones Fans Rock, All 54,000 of Them." By Alan J. Borsuk. *Milwaukee Journal.* June 9, 1975, p. 1.

282. Boston — "The Stones: It's More Than Rock and Roll." By Charlie McCollum. *Washington Star.* June 15, 1975, Calendar, p. 1.

     Major review from Boston Garden, well illustrated, incisive, detailed, with a number of anecdotes and complete show coverage.

283. Cleveland — "Rolling Stones Piling Up Huge Grosses: 840 G in Cleve." *Variety.* June 18, 1975, p. 57.

284. Toronto — "Mick Is Still Mighty and the Stones Superb." *Globe and Mail* (Toronto). June 19, 1975, p. 13.

285. New York — "At Jagger Show, Band Beats to 100 Different Drums." By George Goodman, Jr. *New York Times.* June 25, 1975, p. 28.

     Feature article on the steel drummers who opened the shows at Madison Square Garden.

286. New York — "Camaraderie Unites Fans at Rolling Stones Opener." By Robert McG. Thomas. *New York Times.* June 23, 1975, p. 34.

Report of the scene outside the Garden before the opening-night concert. Emphasizes the scalper's market that existed there, and quotes many young fans' feelings about group.

287. New York — "Madison Fantasy Garden Set for Stones Tomorrow." By John Rockwell. *New York Times.* June 21, 1975, p. 21.

Describes special stage effects planned by Jules Fisher for Madison Square Garden concerts.

288. New York — "Mick Rolls On." By Marian McEvoy. *Women's Wear Daily.* June 24, 1975, pp. 4–5.

Emphasizes fashion notes, Mick's costumes.

289. New York — "Rolling." By Jan Hodenfield. *New York Post.* June 25, 1975, p. 61.

Overview of the band on tour, with capsule character studies of various band members. Concentrates on the Garden concerts and is critical of some aspects of the staging and lighting.

·290. New York — "Rolling Stones Begin 6 Nights at Garden with Finely Crafted Show Before Sold-out House of 19,500." By John Rockwell. *New York Times.* June 24, 1975, p. 21.

Primarily a comparison of Garden show with those the author witnessed previously on the road. Somewhat critical of performance, the author suggests that "maybe the band felt constrained by the new stage or by the first night in New York."

291. New York — "Rolling Stones Start Gathering Moola Moss." By Patricia O'Haire. *Daily News.* June 23, 1975, p. 5.

292. New York — "Stoned." *Daily News.* June 23, 1975, pp. 40–41.

     Centerfold selection of photos from Sunday night opening concert, all excellent.

293. New York — "The Stones." By James Spina. *Women's Wear Daily.* June 24, 1975, p. 20.

     Rave review of Garden concerts. Quote: "This band led by the visual-vocal presence of Mick Jagger and the musical mastery of Keith Richard is a study of infinite growth and upward motion. . . . the music touches on every sphere in the human experience."

294. New York — "The Stones' Descent on the Garden." By Jan Hodenfield. *New York Post.* June 23, 1975, p. 39.

     Generally unfavorable review.

295. New York — "Stones Exit N. Y. in Haze of Glory." By Frank Meyer. *Variety.* July 2, 1975, p. 2.

296. New York — "Stones $1.2 Mil Sellouts in N. Y." By Jim Melanson. *Billboard.* July 5, 1975, p. 22.

297. New York — "Stones Pile Up Big $1,250,000 Gross at Mad. Sq. Garden." *Variety.* June 25, 1975, p. 59.

298. New York — "The Stones Stumble, but Finally Deliver." By Tony Kornheiser. *Newsday.* June 24, 1975, p. 32A.

Quote: "The Rolling Stones are no longer giving concerts. They are priests. They are giving religion." The review concludes that with the encore "Sympathy for the Devil" the band has cleansed itself of whatever stain of Altamont still remained. "The devils were gone. The fallen angels restored."

299. Philadelphia — "Rolling Stones: Still High Voltage." By Jack Lloyd. *Philadelphia Inquirer.* July 1, 1975, Section B, p. 5.

300. Washington — "Ladies and Gentlemen, the Raunchy and Rollin' Stones." By Larry Rohter and Alex Ward. *Washington Post.* July 3, 1975, Section C, p. 3.

Having declared the Stones passé before their arrival, Rohter concludes after viewing their Tuesday night concert that "they are still very much the Rolling Stones. However much their offstage image may have mellowed in recent years, onstage they remain the very personification of tough, raunchy, street punk rock 'n' rollers."

301. Washington —"Rolling Stones (7)." *Variety.* July 9, 1975, p. 62.

302. Washington — "Rolling Stones Gather Some Moss." By Larry Rohter. *Washington Post.* June 29, 1975, Section H, p. 1.

One of those rare instances in which a concert is reviewed before it has occurred. Rohter completely reversed his opinion that the Stones are slipping after witnessing their performance at the Capital Centre three nights later.

303. Los Angeles — "Are the Stones Gathering Moss?" By Robert Hilburn. *Los Angeles Times*, IV, p. 1.

     Hilburn concludes that "the band is less exciting in concert now than in 1969, Jagger is less dynamic on stage, and the band's new material is weaker than the material it introduced on past tours." However, he continues, "the band is still the greatest pure rock group in the world and it's not a hollow championship based on the absence of strong competition." This review is a classic example of the Stones' dilemma — that their only competition is their younger selves. The author's description of the Forum concerts is excellent and includes some amusing anecdotes.

304. Los Angeles — "I'm Mick — Fly Me!" *Los Angeles Free Press.* July 18–24, 1975, pp. 1, 16–17.

     Centerfold montage comprised of fifteen photos from the Forum concerts and brief text covering highlights of the shows.

305. Los Angeles — "Stones — Total Rock." By Harvey Kubernik. *Melody Maker.* July 26, 1975, p. 27.

     Rave review in a British publication whose Los Angeles correspondent states: "Along with the Who they are the two best British imports to visit this country in the last ten years."

306. San Francisco — "The Crowd Got What They Wanted." By Joel Selvin. *San Francisco Chronicle.* July 17, 1975, p. 42.

307. San Francisco — "A Joyous Frenzy at the Cow Palace." By Julie Smith. *San Francisco Chronicle.* July 16, 1975, pp. 1, 30.

308. San Francisco — "132 Minutes of Frenzy with Mick." By Robert Hollis. *San Francisco Examiner.* July 16, 1975, p. 1.

309. Chicago — "Are Rolling Stones Gathering Moss?" By Jack Hafferkamp. *Chicago Daily News.* July 23, 1975, pp. 1, 17.

     The reviewer concludes that the Stones "certainly gave the crowd a double-dose of what it wanted." However, he suggests that this might well be their last tour and that if so he's glad to know "that the Rolling Stones intend to go out with a bang and not a whimper."

310. Chicago — "No Use to Describe Stones." By Al Rudis. *Chicago Sun-Times.* July 23, 1975, p. 73.

     Quote: "How do you write with a blown mind? How do you collect yourself when your body and soul have been shattered? How do you tell someone about rock and roll? How do you tell someone about the Rolling Stones?" How indeed? This is a rave review obviously, and it includes many excellent illustrations.

311. Chicago — "Satisfying Spectacle from Rolling Stones." By Lynn Van Matre. *Chicago Tribune.* July 24, 1975, I, p. 18.

312. Atlanta — "Scalpers Score at Stones Gig: Narcs Do, Too." *Variety.* Aug. 6, 1975, p. 45.

313. Atlanta — "The Stones Hit the Omni." By Art Harris. *The Atlanta Constitution.* July 31, 1975, pp. 1, 18.

    Rave review highlighted by some vignettes of fans and a particularly insightful anecdote about Jagger's acquisition of a painting of himself.

314. Jacksonville — "Delay in Florida." *Variety.* Aug. 13, 1975, p. 47.

315. Buffalo — "Rolling Stones Wind U. S. Tour with Buffalo Gig." *Variety.* Aug. 13, 1975, p. 47.

316. Buffalo — "Stones Farewell at Buff. Stadium." *Variety.* July 30, 1975, p. 53.

Retrospectives

*317. "A Fan's Note." By Mary Pinkham. *Atlantic Monthly.* 236: 81–83. Sept. 1975.

    Recollections of a concert centering on the band's apparent agelessness and the various members' special contributions to the show. There are perceptive comments about the relationship of Jagger, Richard, and Wood.

318. "Flashbacks to the Stones Tour: On the Road to Buffalo." By Lisa Robinson. *Creem.* 8:33–38. Dec. 1975.

    This is an unusually amusing article; it is hard to believe that Jagger's comments are not indeed his comments. When he chats about the press you somehow believe: "I don't read any of the analytical stuff." And, referring to bad reviews he says, "As long as my picture is on the front page, I don't care what they say about me on page 96." Numerous photos of the band.

319. "Jaggernaut: Wild Horse on a Plastic Phallus." By Charles Bukowski. *Creem.* 7:44–46. Oct. 1975.

    Recollections of the Forum concert by a literary figure more interested in the scene than the show. Many fine photos by Neal Preston.

320. "Stones American Diary." *Rock Scene.* 3:10–15. Nov. 1975.

    Photo story of the tour.

321. "Stones' Private Tour Scrapbook." *Rock Scene.* 4:48–58. Jan. 1976.

    Photo story of the tour. Cover shot of Jagger.

322. "Stones '75." *Creem.* 7:33–35. Aug. 1975.

    Photo story of the tour.

The Albums *Made in the Shade* and *Metamorphosis*

*323. "The Recycled Stones: Oldies and Outtakes." By Stephen Davis. *Rolling Stone.* Aug. 14, 1975, pp. 42, 45.

    Made in the Shade is praised briefly as a collection of greatest hits, but *Metamorphosis* is discussed in detail; its value as a historical collection of Stones takes and outtakes is acknowledged. There is considerable enthusiasm for some of these early efforts while others are regarded as flawed. *Metamorphosis* is nevertheless declared to be a "collector's album."

324. "The Rolling Loog Orchestra: *Metamorphosis.*" By Jon Tiven. *Circus Raves.* 2:57. Sept. 1975.

    This reviewer calls the album "the best since *Flowers.*" He also reports that it is selling twice as well as the authorized greatest hits album, *Made in the Shade.*

325. "The Rolling Stones: *Metamorphosis.*" By Lester Bangs. *Creem.* 7:65. Aug. 1975.

    Favorable review: "It's the first thing I've heard in years that reminds me how fine it was to be alive in 1964–65, knowing the Stones were too and living for them if nothing else."

326. "Rolling Stones — *Metamorphosis.*" By Janis Schact. *Circus.* 9:8–9. Sept. 2, 1975.

    The album is praised for its youthful excitement, reminiscent of *Aftermath* and *Flowers.* Although not representative of the band today, it is nevertheless a reminder of the contributions of Brian Jones and Andrew Oldham in the early days.

327. "Stones Launch Onslaught '75 with *Made in the Shade.*" By Dan Nooger. *Circus.* 9:30–35. Aug. 1975.

    Track-by-track analysis of album; the history of each cut is included as well as choice color shots of the Stones in action in Baton Rouge. Cover drawing of Jagger.

*328. "The Stones — on Disc and on Tour." By Steve Simels. *Stereo Review.* 35:86–87. Aug. 1975.

    Favorable reviews of both albums. Simels would have liked some substitutions in *Made in the Shade*, and he cheerfully admits that *Metamorphosis* is typically Stones-sloppy, but he concludes that rock 'n' roll, "the most vital and overwhelming pop music of the 20th century," is here to stay and that the Stones on the road again in the summer of '75 is the best way "to shake us out of our collective doldrums."

1976-1977:

Soul Survivors

As had become their habit, the Stones followed their highly successful American tour with a moderately successful European tour. The smaller halls in Europe lowered profit margins as the band tried to duplicate the massive American experience with all of its special stage effects, vastly expensive to move and to install. The British press remained generally negative, and some planned dates did not materialize for various reasons. The Iron Curtain countries retained their iron stand against any intrusions by the "decadent" Rolling Stones.

Keith was arrested again in Britain on drug charges, and although he was released with a token fine, his record was once again sullied in the eyes of American immigration officials. A few months later, in Toronto, he was arrested again. This time the charge was truly frightening. Keith himself called it "my first real bust" as he faced trial for trafficking in heroin. For the first time the possibility of a long-term jail sentence threatened not only Keith's freedom but also the continued viability of the Stones as a performing group, for to perform without Keith would be unthinkable.

Just two days after the arrest the Stones carried out a planned appearance at a small Toronto club in order to record a live session before an invited audience. The El Mocambo set appeared on the new album *Love You Live* — along with live tracks from the European tour — and was considered by many critics to be the high point of the two-disc offering. The album received generally favorable reviews.

At the end of 1977 Keith remained in deep trouble with Canadian authorities. At the same time rumors abounded regarding a 1978 American tour. The Stones had been in trouble before; early in their careers there was even a song called "Blame It on the Stones." From trouble they had inevitably drawn strength. Could they do it again?

*329. *The Rolling Stones.* By Tony Jasper. [London, Octopus Books Ltd., 1976.]

Especially attractive book with marvelous color photographs, "chronicles the story of Mick Jagger, Keith Richard, Charlie Watts, Bill Wyman and the late Brian Jones month by month and year by year, gives details of all who have been associated with them and their extraordinary careers, and analyzes how the Rolling Stones have been able to maintain their success . . . over such a long period."

*330. *The Rolling Stones: An Illustrated Record.* By Roy Carr. New York, Harmony Books, [1976].

Can only be called an incredible achievement. Just about every fact you have ever wanted to know about the band is included: history, discography, filmography, bootleg records, tours, album covers (full-page and in color) plus numerous photos, most of which have not appeared previously. Even tour posters are included. This book could only have been done with the Stones' cooperation.

331. "Hot Stuff from Mick and Keith." By Chet Flippo. *Rolling Stone.* Nov. 3, 1977, pp. 13, 17–19.

     Mick discusses *Love You Live*, indicates humorous approval of Johnny Rotten and the Sex Pistols, humorous disapproval of the "Rock Music Awards" television special. Keith talks about his upcoming drug trial in Canada and about the controversial Robert Frank film *Cocksucker Blues.*

332. "The Last Time? With the Stones in Toronto." By Lisa Robinson. *Hit Parader.* Sept. 1977, pp. 28–30.

     Splendid account of the El Mocambo shows emphasizing the art of Mick Jagger; illustrated with photos taken at the club. Margaret Trudeau's presence at the club and at the Stones' hotel is mentioned.

333. "Margaret in Wonderland." By David Cobb. *MacLean's.* Mar. 21, 1977, pp. 63–66.

     One of several articles on Margaret Trudeau's association with the band in Toronto, but made special by its color photographs of the group performing at the El Mocambo.

334. "Robert Frank Screens the Stones' Blue Movie." By Merrill Shindler. *Rolling Stone.* Dec. 30, 1976, pp. 19–20.

     Description of a San Francisco showing of *Cocksucker Blues,* the difficulties preventing its release, Frank's comments about his film and about the '72 tour, "a hard trip to survive."

335. "Rolling Stones Back Off from 'Mini-Tour'." *Rolling Stone.* July 15, 1976, p. 10.

Official notice that the planned bicentennial tour of America, involving six cities, was cancelled. The group cited exhaustion after the European tour as the prime reason for the cancellation.

336. "Rolling Stones Concert on Easter Island Rejected." *New York Times.* Dec. 14, 1975, p. 73.

The Chilean government decides against a proposed Stones concert on Easter Island "because the whole future of the island was going to be damaged." About one hundred thousand rock music fans were expected.

337. "The Rolling Stones Return to Roots with Rare Club Date." By John Rockwell. *Washington Star.* Mar. 7, 1977, p. A8.

Perceptive account of the El Mocambo show. Rockwell stresses that in the small space of the 350-seat club "the great Stones came across tighter and tougher than ever before." Of Jagger's performance he says, "Up close the man's wit and teasing cleverness came across in a way they can never do in an arena." He adds an ominous footnote — that Richard's drug bust a week prior to the show might presage the end of the band should he be convicted.

338. "The Rolling Stones Think Small." By John Rockwell. *New York Times.* Mar. 7, 1977, p. 27.

Review of the El Mocambo show by the rock music critic of the *Times.* Discussing Richard's trial and possible imprisonment, Rockwell concludes: "Given the energy, conviction and sheer joy here, it was almost impossible to believe that this could be the end of anything."

339. "Stones Re-sign with Atlantic." *Rolling Stone.* Apr. 21, 1977, p. 15.

    Brief account of the Stones' new contract with Atlantic; update on Keith Richard's hearing for possession of cocaine and for trafficking in heroin.

340. "The Trouble with *Cocksucker Blues.*" *Rolling Stone.* Nov. 3, 1977, p. 18.

    Brief note outlining the arrangement between Robert Frank and the Stones which permits limited viewing of the film, a pseudodocumentary of the 1972 American tour.

European Tour (1976)

341. "Rolling Stones at the Fair: Nuffin' from Nuffin' . . ." By Mick Brown. *Rolling Stone.* Oct. 7, 1976, pp. 12, 25.

    Report on the concert at Knebworth Fair, the largest audience the band had played to since Altamont. However, unlike that ill-fated festival, this time the crowd was well behaved and the mood upbeat.

342. "Stones in Germany — World Next?" By Paul Gambaccini. *Rolling Stone.* June 3, 1976, pp. 10, 12.

    Review of the Frankfurt concert which includes some comments by Jagger about returning to the academic life. He says, "It's kind of limiting, in a way, using your intellect to write songs like 'Brown Sugar'."

343. "Stones Roll Over Europe." By Gary Herman. *Circus.* July 22, 1976, pp. 30–31.

Brief account, but replete with facts and figures on the European jaunt. Photos of Mick in action.

344. "Stones Tour Europe." *Rock Scene.* 4:31–36. Nov. 1976.

Photo coverage of European tour.

*345. "To Rolled to Stone?" By Charles Shaar Murray. *Creem.* 8:50–55. Aug. 1976.

Lively account of the Frankfurt concert with excellent color photographs. The author is cheerfully irreverent in his description of the group's onstage and offstage activities.

The Album *Black and Blue*

346. "*Black and Blue* — The Rolling Stones." By Paul Nelson. *Circus.* July 22, 1976, p. 12.

Favorable review in which Nelson refuses to compare the album to previous works such as *Exile* which he regards as "their certified masterpiece." He compares the Stones to Muhammad Ali in that they fight just hard enough to win and to retain their title. He selects "Memory Motel" as the best cut and, assuming that Jagger is as biographical as usual, he wonders who among his many loves he is referring to. About Jagger he says, "there might be just a few more tomorrows but there certainly have been a lot of tough yesterdays."

347. "*Black & Blue*: Tongue in Cheek Mick Jagger Talks to Lisa Robinson." By Lisa Robinson. *Hit Parader Annual.* Winter 1976–77, pp. 6, 67–69.

Jagger discusses the new album on his way from the Caribbean to Europe, refusing to be serious about a single cut. He talks about his collaboration with Keith on their songs and about the costumes he will be wearing on the European tour.

*348. "Glimmer Twins Star as Stones Roll On." By Dave Marsh. *Rolling Stone.* May 20, 1976, pp. 63–64.

Favorable review including track-by-track analysis. Marsh concludes that the Stones are "soul survivors" indeed; Jagger's vocals and certain outstanding instrumentals make up for what he regards as relatively weak songs that rely too much on loose riffs which lack organization and control.

349. "Only *Black & Blue*, but They Like It." By Chet Flippo. *Rolling Stone.* May 6, 1976, pp. 10, 12.

Mick J. discusses the new album track by track and also the upcoming European tour. He declines to predict when he will retire.

*350. "The Rolling Stones: *Black and Blue*: Two Points of View." By Dave Hickey and James Wolcott. *Circus.* June 1, 1976, pp. 26–31.

Hickey finds *Black and Blue* to be typical Stones, lowdown and eminently enjoyable in its funkiness. "Since Altamont they have been almost relentless in their insistence on being taken for exactly what they are: a damn good rock & roll band making a lot of money, putting on a good show doing what they like to do." He also sees the album as another step in the "systematic demystification" which has taken place since the "artsy-studio magic of *Satanic Majesties*" and the "demagoguery of Altamont." Wolcott finds the album shallow and disappointing and conjectures that the Stones have deteriorated into a bunch of session men now bereft of the genius that illuminated their earlier works. He pays tribute to the great body of work which did give us "satisfaction" and hopes that in some forthcoming tour they will once again "kick us like they kicked us before." Excellent color photos including cover photo of Mick and Keith.

351. "The Stones: *Black and Blue.*" By Steve Simels. *Stereo Review.* 37:92. July 1976.

Simels expresses pleasure in the Stones' pronounced return to their rhythm and blues roots. Although he acknowledges some weak tracks, he feels that the album is the best since *Exile*, that it will be *the* rock and roll statement of 1976.

The Album *Love You Live*

*352. " 'It's Time for More Energy in Music,' Say The Rolling Stones." By John Rockwell. *New York Times.* Oct. 9, 1977, II, pp. 21, 28.

Very favorable review in which Rockwell declares the album to be the best live offering ever produced by the band which is, he believes, "at the peak of its skills." He discusses in detail the group's rhythm and blues roots and applauds the work of Ron Wood in enhancing their raw, tight sound. On the question of image, Jagger and Richard express monumental indifference.

*353. "Live Stones: Almost What We Wanted." By Paul Nelson. *Rolling Stone*. Nov. 17, 1977, pp. 81–85.

Favorable review in which Nelson emphasizes that one's expectations — that every Stones album emerge as a certified masterpiece — is patently unfair. He is especially pleased with the El Mocambo set and concludes that "what's here this minute is quite memorable in its own right."

*354. "Not Fade Away." By Patrick Carr. *New Times*. 9:75. Oct. 28, 1977.

This reviewer commends the album for its ability to re-create the communal experience of a concert with its "tension, density and craziness." But his real excitement is elicited by the El Mocambo side, in his own words, "the hardest, funniest, most inspiring rock and roll record in years." Here the essence of the Stones is experienced in its most effective setting, the smoky, sweaty club scene. Carr looks forward to the next studio album on the basis of the vitality expressed on this album.

Personalities

Articles and news items on the Stones, other than Jagger, are few. This in no way invalidates their worth as essential ingredients in the Stones sound, but it does make them a poor source for the kind of personality analysis to which superstars are eternally subjected. Most items that feature the Stones as individuals are articles written about a particular event, such as the Hyde Park concert, Altamont, the release of a new album, etc. Therefore, most of the items in this section are interviews in which the personality of the man is given prime focus. The list is small because, other than Jagger, The Rolling Stones are treated as a group; the possible exceptions are Keith, who is developing an identifiable persona, and Brian, who died before his uniqueness could be fully realized.

*355. "Bill Wyman off Bass." By Bruce Malamut. *Crawdaddy.* Aug. 1974, pp. 55–60.

Extensive article obviously based on a very long interview. Wyman discusses his way of life, musical interests, his fellow Stones, all very frankly. Also some discussion of his solo album, *Monkey Grip.* Illustrated with photos of Bill.

356. "Bill Wyman Solo: It's Me, Such As I Am." By Andrew Bailey. *Rolling Stone.* June 6, 1974, p. 16.

Conversations with Bill about his record *Monkey Grip.*

*357. "Brian Jones: Sympathy for the Devil." By Greil Marcus. *Rolling Stone.* Aug. 9, 1969, pp. 1, 6–8.

Memorial tribute to Brian — recapitulates his career, discusses circumstances of his death and contributing factors in his personal and professional life. A number of interesting photos.

358. "Brian Was a Rolling Stone." By Toby Goldstein. *Rock.* July 23, 1973, pp. 24–25.

A fan's reminiscences about Brian. Good illustrations of Brian and the early Stones.

359. "Charlie Watts: A Stone Left Unturned." By Ben Sidran. *Words & Music.* 2:28–31. June 1972.

Articles about Charlie Watts are rare and this is a good one. Charlie discusses his interest in jazz primarily. Also included are thoughtful comments by Jagger about Watts.

*360. "For a Song." By Jim Jerome. *People.* 8:55–58 Nov. 21, 1977.

Intimate look at the Stones' musical mastermind, Keith Richard, as he awaits court decision on his most serious drug bust. Keith discusses his habit frankly, claiming that he has given up hard drugs and talking about his current priorities and plans. Jagger is also quoted about his family and about his goals at age thirty-four. Many photos including cover photo of Mick and Keith.

361. "Gettin' a Bit Intimate 'Ere, I Dunno If *Zigzag* Can Take All This . . . Keith Richard." By Nick Kent. *Zigzag.* 5:26–32. No. 47. (This issue not dated.)

    Very frank interview with Keith in which he discusses recording in Jamaica, drug busts, and various other performers such as Chuck Berry, Jack Nietzche, Little Richard, the Ronettes, etc. Fine photographs, including cover photo of Keith.

362. "Keith Richard." By Ritchie Yorke. *Rolling Stone.* Nov. 15, 1969, p. 18.

    In an interview Keith discusses forthcoming recording ventures, the Stones' need to remain a touring band, and Mick's entry into films, among other topics.

363. "Keith Richard: A Few Words with the Exile." By Billy Walker and Jack Hutton. *Rock.* Aug. 13, 1973, pp. 16–17.

    Conversation with Keith about recording in Jamaica and the new album, *Goats Head Soup.* Cover photo of Keith.

364. "Keith Richard Busted: Stones' Future Cloudy." By Chet Flippo. *Rolling Stone.* Apr. 7, 1977, p. 17.

    Detailed coverage of the Richard drug arrest in Toronto; gloom and doom is predicted. The possibility of Keith's receiving a long prison sentence is considered.

*365. "Keith Richard Caught Live: A Long Look at The Rolling Stones' *Love You Live*, and the Journey Between Then and Now." By Paul Nelson. *Circus.* Sept. 29, 1977, pp. 24–28.

Revealing chat with Keith about the El Mocambo show, the difference between the sixties and the seventies, the friendship between the Stones and the Beatles, Keith's work habits, his drug bust and subsequent detoxification. Many color photos of Keith and the band, cover photo of Keith.

366. "Keith Richard Guilty: 'I'm Just Relieved'." *Rolling Stone.* Feb. 24, 1977, p. 15.

Brief account of Keith's conviction on January 11, 1977, for cocaine possession in England.

*367. "Keith Richard: Heroin, Old Age, Rhythm and Blues." By Victor Bockris. *High Times.* Jan. 1978, pp. 24–31.

Long, outstanding interview with Keith who is obviously comfortable with this publication and supercooperative with his interviewer. He is unusually eloquent on a variety of topics including his recent drug difficulties in Canada. An added bonus is a profusion of color photographs of Keith looking suitably wasted.

*368. "Keith Richard Meets the Mounties and Faces the Music." By Chet Flippo. *Rolling Stone.* May 5, 1977, pp. 49–55.

Very detailed account of Keith's drug bust in Toronto. The El Mocambo shows are also covered and there is considerable conjecture regarding the band's future in light of the seriousness of the charges against Keith. Photos by Annie Leibowitz.

*369. "Keith Richard Soul Survivor: An Old Dog Gets New Teeth." By Patrick Carr. *New Times.* 9:70–73. Oct. 28, 1977.

Keith is described as "the eternal punk, the sullen kid who only wants to play rock 'n' roll and be left alone by the squares. In this guise he is almost impossibly hip." Carr discusses a number of topics with Keith: his drug bust, the album *Love You Live*, his physical health (Keith claims that he has a very strong constitution), his family, and his reading habits. This is a fascinating glimpse of a fascinating man. Color portrait of Keith and guitar at home in Westchester.

370. "Keith Richard: 'The Pusher' Behind the Stones." By Barbara Charone. *Creem.* 8:37–39. Oct. 1976.

Interview with Keith in Scotland. He discusses the album *Black and Blue* and the roles played by various band members. Color photos of Keith. Cover photo of Mick and Keith onstage.

371. "Mick Taylor: The Newest Stone Talks." By Penny Valentine. *Rock.* July 3, 1972, p. 10.

Interview with Taylor in which he discusses *Exile* and the forthcoming American tour, among other topics.

372. "Mick Taylor: The Stone Who Got Away." By Mick Brown. *Rolling Stone.* Nov. 3, 1977, p. 19.

Taylor discusses his activities since leaving the group, his plans for the future. He refers to himself as "the first man to leave the Rolling Stones and live."

*373. "Over His Dead Body." By Al Aronowitz. *No One Waved Good-bye: A Casualty Report on Rock and Roll.* Edited by Robert Somma. New York, Outerbridge and Dienstfrey, [1971], pp. 72–80.

Report on the death of Brian Jones by a friend. The author discusses Brian's character and possible factors contributing to his tragic death. A number of anecdotes illustrate Brian's personality and those of the people surrounding him.

*374. "Present at the Creation." By Lisa Robinson. *Creem.* 8:25–28. June 1976.

"An exclusive interview with Ian Stewart, the Real Sixth Rolling Stone on a Decade and a Half in the Stones Brigade." "Stu" offers historical footnotes regarding the period of the early sixties that only he could provide. He comments about the relationship between Mick, Keith, and Andrew Oldham, discusses Brian Jones's leave-taking, the arrival of Mick Taylor and Ron Wood. Also talks about Mick Jagger's role as group leader and overall financial boss.

*375. "Pulling Teeth with Keith Richard: A Study in Elegant Waste." By Peter Erskine. *Creem.* 6:52–55. Dec. 1974.

Interview with Keith in which he discusses his recent arrest for unlawful possession of drugs and firearms. Other topics include Tony Scaduto's book about Jagger (which he dislikes), Brian Jones, and Keith's dental difficulties. Remarkable article, fun to read.

*376. "The Rolling Stone Interview: Keith Richard." By Robert Greenfield. *Rolling Stone.* Aug. 19, 1971, pp. 24–36.

This is probably the most extensive interview with Keith ever published. It was recorded over a period of several days and is liberally illustrated with photos. Keith discusses nearly every topic one could wish for, including the Stones' recent activities and future plans. He also talks about his drug bust and his relationships with Mick and Brian.

377. "A Rolling Stone Who Gathers No Moss." By Robert Hilburn. *Los Angeles Times.* May 26, 1974, Calendar, p. 54.

Rare interview with Bill Wyman in which he discusses his solo album *Monkey Grip* and also what it is like to play with the premiere rock 'n' roll band. The self-effacing Wyman says that he is happy to allow Jagger the spotlight and explains his need to express himself more as a composer.

*378. "Rolling Stones Are Born Not Made." By Dave Marsh. *Rolling Stone.* Nov. 3, 1977, pp. 72–77.

Excellent article on Ron Wood, outlining his early history as a rocker, his years with the Faces, his decision to join the Stones. Includes a description of Ron jamming with Keith while Mick worked on the mix of *Love You Live.* Photos by Annie Leibowitz.

379. "The Stone Alone Speaks: Here Comes Rhymin' Wyman." By Robert Palmer. *Rolling Stone.* Mar. 25, 1976, p. 10.

Discussion with Bill Wyman regarding his solo album *Stone Alone.* Bill affirms his decision not to seek a solo career.

380. "Stones Section." *Hit Parader.* 80:38–43. Mar. 1971.

   Fairly long interview with Keith Richard and Mick Jagger combined with photos of them in a worthwhile article. Keith is very articulate about their music, also discusses such touchy topics as Brian Jones, the Beatles, other performing groups.

381. "Talking with Keith Richard." By Lenny Berman. *Rock.* May 8, 1972, pp. 12–13.

   Interview with Keith before the start of the 1972 American tour. At a rented house in Bel Air, California, Keith discusses his musical directions, recording techniques, bootleg albums, method of writing songs. Very articulate, relaxed interview in a domestic setting. Cover photo of Keith.

382. "What Makes Billy Swim?" By Kevin Doyle. *Creem.* 7:42–44. May 1976.

   Bill Wyman discusses his role as a Stone, his new album *Stone Alone*, growing old, and his identity apart from the band.

Mick Jagger

.

Mick Jagger, group leader and lead vocalist, is a child of tomorrow, whose complex, multilevel personality will be better understood by succeeding generations than by his own. Certain of his qualities have been established without doubt — he is brutally honest and he has unshakable musical integrity. His performing self seems somehow separate from his real self — his androgynous qualities have been both derided and celebrated. His stage persona is a combination of manner and appearance that attracts and repels with unreasonable force. He is loved and hated in equally unreasonable measure; in their almost unreal loathing of him, his critics disclose the full measure of his power and influence. His face, like no other on earth, according to "critic-at-large" David Littlejohn, is actually disturbing to some people. Why is the "2000 man" so worshipped and reviled, why is he compared alternately to Christ or Satan? Much remains to be known about Jagger, as well as about his time.

In his interviews Jagger discloses little about himself; he is occasionally articulate, but only when he chooses to be, one suspects. His life-style is shrouded; despite a proliferation of anecdotes, his privacy is seldom really disturbed. He talks readily enough about music, generally shies away from politics, religion, world problems. Of his own depths he discloses nothing — perhaps there is nothing to disclose — perhaps his aura of fascination is rooted solely in his performing self — perhaps he is one of our greatest actors.

Jagger's entrance into films has been less than auspicious. Despite brilliant acting on his part, *Performance* was more than most people, even critics, could cope with. *Ned Kelly* was disappointing to Jagger, and one questions casting him in the role of a tough outlaw. But he does have undeniable charisma on screen, despite the uncertainty of his role potential. The question is not, Can Jagger cope with films? but rather, Can the films cope with Jagger?

*383. *Mick Jagger: Everybody's Lucifer.* By Tony Scaduto. New York, David McKay Company, Inc., [1974].

Worth reading despite deficiencies, chiefly the admission by the author that the book is largely fiction. The obvious weakness was Scaduto's inability to interview Jagger himself, or even those nearest to him at this time. The book is very ambitious, covering the period from Jagger's youth to the present. The sources are primarily musicians who knew Jagger in his younger days and the women in his life: Chrissie Shrimpton, Marianne Faithfull, and others, but not Bianca. Therefore, despite the volume of material presented, the question of credibility runs througout the entire text. Many fine illustrations.

*384. *Mick Jagger: The Singer, Not the Song.* By J. Marks. New York, Curtis Books, [1973].

A book that is difficult to characterize. It includes material on Jagger's life, descriptions of concerts and backstage activities in 1972, and a running series of vignettes of various types of Stones freaks, either real or provided by the author's imagination. The overall effect is powerful and although very personal, the book is still exclusively about Jagger and therefore not to be overlooked. Many illustrations, mainly concert photos.

385. "All the Way in St. Tropez." *Rolling Stone*. June 10, 1971, pp. 1, 20.

Detailed account of the wedding of Mick and Bianca in May 1971. Text is humorous, but friendly. Includes a list of wedding guests and some excellent photos.

386. "And Then Elvis Said: I Never Made No Dirty Body Movements." *Crawdaddy*. 4:29. No. 8. (This issue not dated.)

Analysis of Mick's dancing style. Quote: "There is absolutely no way of defining the insinuation, hostility and bravado of Mick's dancing. . . . Mick does not dance to the music; he *is* the music."

387. " 'ave You Seen Your Father?" By Judith Martin. *Washington Post*. July 30, 1974, Section B, p. 1.

Conversation with Professor Joe Jagger about his famous son, chiefly centered on his boyhood, his family background. He indicates that both sides of the family had displayed musical talent.

388. "Bianca! Mrs. Jagger Talks to Andy Warhol and Viva!" *Interview*. Aug. 1972, pp. 7–11.

Among other topics, Bianca discusses her honeymoon with Mick in Morocco, their daughter Jade, and Mick's possible involvement in films.

389. "Bianca Says She Loves Him, Mick Isn't Talking: Is Their Marriage Inert or in Ruins?" *People*. 9:26–27. Feb. 27, 1978.

Gossipy speculations regarding the Jagger marriage, photos of Mick and Bianca, Bianca and Halston, Mick and his latest, model Jerry Hall.

390. " 'A Change Is As Good As a Rest, My Dear': *Rock* Talks to Mick Jagger in London." By Steve Peacock. *Rock.* July 3, 1972, pp. 16–17.

Conversation with Jagger prior to his 1972 American tour. He discusses the album *Exile on Main Street* and his future in films.

391. "The Confessions of Marianne Faithfull: As Years Go By." By Andrew Tyler. *Creem.* 6:44–47. June 1974.

Marianne Faithfull's life is irrevocably intertwined with the development of Mick and the Stones. Her reminiscences of her life with Jagger are always important.

392. "The Decline of Rock." By David Seay. *Crawdaddy.* 4:28. Nov. 7. (This issue not dated.)

Brief but valuable analysis of "evil" in the Stones' music and in the personality of Jagger himself. His voice and singing style are analyzed for their suitability to blues. The Stones' and especially Jagger's musical techninques are used to illustrate the author's premise that the group's image grew out of its music.

393. "Deep Lip: The Mick Jagger Interview, Part 1." By Roy Carr. *Creem.* 6:42–47. July 1974.

Particularly fine two-part interview covering the whole of Jagger's career. In Part 1 he talks about his childhood, early days with the group, and about Brian. Many photos, including cover from their *Between the Buttons* days.

394. "Deep Lip: The Mick Jagger Interview, Part 2." By Roy Carr. *Creem*. 6:52–55. Aug. 1974.

Jagger discusses "the business, the people, and the effect that both have had on his mental and physical equilibrium."

395. "The Demon Prince." *Radio Times*. Apr. 7–13, 1973, pp. 58–60.

Quote: "Mick Jagger on being a father — and Joe Jagger on being Mick's dad." This joint interview is valuable in assessing the "real" Mick Jagger. His parents' comments are always worthwhile because, although they may not be entirely objective, they are never bedazzled. Mick's own comments about daughter Jade betray a facet of his personality, that of concerned father, that is not usually revealed. Cover photo of the young Mick.

396. "Dietrich & the Devil." By John Calendo. *Interview*. Oct. 1972, pp. 26–30.

Comparison of Marlene Dietrich and Mick Jagger! Totally fascinating two-part series. The first part covers Dietrich's career while posing the hypothesis: "In the Atomic Age, Mick Jagger would carry on the Dietrich tradition."

397. "Dietrich & the Devil (Part Two)." By John Calendo. *Interview*. Nov. 1972, pp. 22–23.

Discusses Jagger as this age's counterpart to Dietrich. The author explains that like Dietrich, "Jagger had aligned his presence with an atmosphere of destruction and illegal sex." He talks about Jagger's musical and film careers, ending with some rather wild but interesting conclusions about why "the screen's leading transexual is no longer a woman." Obviously there is a major emphasis on Jagger's role in *Performance*.

398. "The Fop Element." By Betty Byrd. *Crawdaddy*. 6:27. July 4, 1971.

Provocative comments about Jagger as the quintessential fop of rock.

*399. "For a Song: Jagger Wails, Bianca Sails as the Rolling Stones Set Out to Win the West Again." By Jim Jerome. *People*. 3:18–22. June 9, 1975.

Splendid though casual portrait of Jagger with lively, informative text that concentrates less on his past history, more on Jagger now, his complex personality, his relationship with his wife. Quotes from both Mick and Bianca are particularly interesting and the photos are outstanding, including fine cover portrait of Jagger.

400. "France: Pagan Event." *Newsweek*. 77:36. May 24, 1971.

Wedding report, with background notes on Mick's attitude toward marriage and society in general as expressed in earlier interviews. Detailed description of the marriage ceremonies, and events before and after. Short but pungent comments on the affair and its participants.

*401. "Head Stone." By Alan Corey. *Playboy*. 16:162–164. Nov. 1969.

Highly intelligent article, chiefly concerned with the Stones' and particularly Jagger's effect on the mores of modern England. Contains one of the few really articulate interviews in which Jagger's philosophy of life is allowed to emerge as well as his ideas on politics and protest. One of the most revealing articles regarding his own personality.

*402. "I Used to Think I Was Really Ugly." By Fred Newman. *The Age of Rock.* Edited by Jonathan Eisen. New York, Vintage Books, [1969], pp. 103–108.

Excellent interview in which Mick speaks clearly, even eloquently regarding his emotions, his stage persona, his feelings toward women, marriage, life in general. Very revealing in terms of his view of himself as a man and of his role as a rock superstar.

*403. " 'I Want to Go Out on a Limb: The Mick Jagger Interview." By Barbara Charone. *Crawdaddy.* Aug. 1976, pp. 32–40.

This is an impressive interview conducted after a concert in the wee hours of the morning. Jagger talks about the band, its music, its future, and about his own film aspirations. His manner is unnerving to his interviewer who concludes that "even constantly-wasted Keith Richard is more energetic in conversation." Jagger's aloofness is classically expressed in his comments on "Rolling Stones casualties." Mick says, "Nothing is permanent and no one is irreplaceable. You can't expect to work with people *forever.*" Perhaps Jagger's distance is necessary to his sanity. Many photos of Mick in performance and offstage; also cover photo.

404. "Jagger and the Stones." By Bruce Cook. *Commonweal.* 102:212–214. June 20, 1975.

Thoughtful study of the Jagger persona, his aura of apparent evil onstage and in his screen portrayal of Turner in *Performance*. Comments on Anthony Scaduto's biography of Jagger (which he takes seriously — see entry 383). In a discussion of Altamont, Cook says: "We shall have to understand the appeal of Mick Jagger and the Rolling Stones if we are to understand the nature of violence and mass hysteria in our time and the one to come."

405. "Jagger Backstage." By Lisa Robinson. *Hit Parader Annual.* Winter 1975, pp. 48–50.

Series of anecdotes about Jagger and friends after Eric Clapton's Garden concert. Color photos of Jagger.

406. "Jagger: Do the Media Have the Message?" By Robert Hilburn. *Los Angeles Times.* June 22, 1975, Calendar, pp. 1, 66.

Long interview with Mick which is exceptionally effective and lucid. The questions are intelligent and Mick's answers are thoughtful and complete. He discusses his media image, the Stones' recent albums, his preferences among rock performers, his co-writing chores with Keith, his film career, and the Stones' plans for the future.

*407. "Jagger Jaw Session: Mannish Boy Gets What He . . . Needs." By Barbara Charone. *Creem.* 9:42–45. Jan. 1978.

Long interview with Mick covering tour plans, album *Love You Live*, Keith's drug arrest, the punk rock scene, Mick's own preferences in Stones albums, and the next studio album. Jagger is realistic about fans' expectations and the Stones' ability or inability to satisfy them. He concedes that recent albums have been called "transitional" because not every cut was considered successful. He agrees that all cuts should be good and states that the Stones do their best in this regard. He identifies as his personal favorites the Stones' first album and *Beggars Banquet*. Many illustrations, cover photo of Jagger.

408. "Jaggers." By Claude De Leusse. *Women's Wear Daily*. May 17, 1971, p. 5.

In its own inimitable way, WWD covers Mick's wedding. Coverage includes rather tongue-in-cheek commentary, some excellent photographs of various participants, including Mick's friends and relatives.

409. "Just Call Me Mick." *Hit Parader*. 78:18–21. July 1970.

Brief account of Mick's starring roles in *Performance* and *Ned Kelly*. Valuable for its contrasting shots of Mick as the virile Ned and as the androgynous Turner.

410. "Marianne Faithfull: Ophelia Goes Home to Mother." By Nik Cohn. *Nova*. Apr. 1971, pp. 52–55.

Interesting sidelights on Jagger are revealed in this extensive article on his former mistress, which recapitulates her abortive career and her life before and after Jagger. Some photos of Mick and Marianne are included.

411. "Mick." By Alfred G. Aronowitz. *New York Post*. July 24, 1972.

Famous pop music writer reminisces about his friendship with Jagger beginning in 1964. Talks about Mick's relationship with Brian and, after Altamont, Mick's developing maturity and responsibility.

*412. "Mick Jagger." *Current Biography*. Dec. 1972, pp. 18–21.

Excellent biographical sketch in an impeccable source. Unmistakable recognition of Jagger's accomplishments.

413. "Mick Jagger." *Mademoiselle*. 71:102. July 1970.

Brief but keen comments on the emergence of Mick's various stage personalities, from gutter boy to unisexual idol. Explores the development of his appeal from girls to girls *and* boys.

414. "Mick Jagger." By John Carpenter. *Los Angeles Free Press*. July 26, 1968, p. 36.

Brief, but contains a degree of intimacy not usually present in Jagger interviews. Discussion topics: the Stones' drug problems, the movie *Sympathy for the Devil*, and the Stones' live concert at the Pops Festival in England.

415. "Mick Jagger." By Jonathan Cott and Sue Clark. *The Rolling Stone Interviews*. By the editors of *Rolling Stone*. New York, Paperback Library, [1971], pp. 158–171.

"Completed in June 1968 at the Rolling Stones' business offices in London. . . . Although it is not the most thorough and complete set of questions and answers it was nonetheless the most extensive discussion then available with Mick Jagger about the Rolling Stones." Very worthwhile interview, though not Mick at his most articulate.

416. "Mick Jagger." By Gloria Stavers. *Celebrity*. 1:38–41. July 1975.

Despite inaccuracies, this is a lively overview of Jagger's career, liberally illustrated with photos of Jagger at May

1 "mini-concert" in New York, and with various of his ladies. Includes a number of interesting quotes about Jagger from friends and acquaintances.

*417. "Mick Jagger and the Future of Rock." By S. K. Oberbeck. *Newsweek.* 77:44–48. Jan. 4, 1971.

This article is a *must,* the most powerful and informative discourse at that time on Jagger and The Rolling Stones. Inclusive, carefully researched, it provides material on almost every facet of the group's history and of Jagger's personality. There are a number of illustrations, all excellent and a cover photo of Mick.

*418. "Mick Jagger & The Nature of Rock." By William Bowling Hedgepeth. *Intellectual Digest.* 3:45–47. Nov. 1972.

Beginning with a vivid description of the impact of a Stones concert on an audience, the author then delves into rock's origins in rhythm and blues, the history of the Stones and concludes with a sociological analysis of the band's role in modern society. The author admits "people are different now, rock has been a catalyst that's helped to change the shape of things." But he is ambivalent, noting that while "psychic distances between people have been shrinking, that males and females have been freed from rigidly polarized roles . . . we've all become part of the same tribe." Cover is an extraordinary sculpture of Jagger by George Guisti.

*419. "Mick Jagger and The Rolling Stones: An Analysis of Their Mystique." By David Littlejohn. Educational television program, presented Nov. 5 and 6, 1971.

Mr. Littlejohn, "critic-at-large," has created a profound and exciting fifteen-minute program which reviews the Stones' career while focusing on the personality of Mick Jagger. He stresses the impact of the Stones on society and the validity of the musical creativity and stage artistry that has been their hallmark. The program includes scenes from the films *Gimme Shelter* and *Performance*.

420. "Mick Jagger As Hard-Working Playboy." By Steve Peacock. *Rock.* Nov. 19, 1973, pp. 20–21.

Conversation with Jagger prior to 1972 American tour, primarily about music rather than about his private life. Jagger tries to debunk his playboy image. Illustrations of Jagger at Nicaragua benefit.

*421. "Mick Jagger: Biography, Part 1." By J. Marks. *Zoo World.* Nov. 22, 1973, pp. 12–13.

Excerpts from J. Marks's book *Mick Jagger.* Cover photo of Jagger.

*422. "Mick Jagger: Biography, Part 2." By J. Marks. *Zoo World.* Dec. 6, 1973, pp. 10, 42–43.

Continued excerpts from J. Marks's book *Mick Jagger.*

423. "Mick Jagger Calls on Me." By David Felton. *Rolling Stone.* Oct. 9, 1975, p. 63.

In meeting his idol the author is so deliberately supercool that he's downright rude. It isn't clear whether this is a real or an imaginary encounter. In any case it is an interesting comment on the difficulty fans have in relating to superstars, and perhaps, the sheer impossibility of superstars relating succesfully to fans.

*424. "Mick Jagger — 'I Can Get It Up, but I Can't Get It Down'." By David Marsh. *Creem.* 7:36–39. Aug. 1975.

Informal interview which took place in Montauk prior to the first concert in 1975. Jagger discusses his plans for the tour and subsequent tours in parts of the world that the Stones haven't visited. He talks about his desire to stay out of politics and confesses that he now feels more American than British. Color photo of Mick is one of the best, and the issue features cover photo of Mick and Keith. (Jagger also reports on his recent attempts to learn to fly an airplane.)

*425. "Mick Jagger, I Love You." By Helen Lawrenson. *Esquire.* 71:132–135. June 1969.

One of the most informative and illuminating articles ever published on Jagger. Lawrenson's perceptive account is alternately humorous and serious. Covers history of the Stones, comments on the drug trial in 1967, provides description of the filming of *Performance*, and most important, contains many in-depth interviews with Jagger which are unusually revealing in tone and content.

426. "Mick Jagger on Ego Trips and Image." By Michael Satchell. *Washington Star.* June 1, 1975, p. 1.

Very long interview with Mick in New York just prior to his departure for Baton Rouge. Mick discusses his view of himself fairly candidly, also talks about the selection of songs for the tour, his feelings toward America, drugs, and his future plans.

427. "Mick Jagger: On Rockin' and Rollin' and Running Around." By Victor Bockris. *Celebrity.* 3:8–10. Sept. 1977.

    Mick and Bianca are presented as a jet-set couple. Jagger discusses his future, also rock and roll wives ("all dreadful"). Bianca calls Mick "the smartest man I ever met." Both explain how their seven-year-old marriage has survived.

428. "Mick Jagger Says . . ." By John Carpenter. *Los Angeles Free Press.* Nov. 21, 1969, p. 33.

    Slightly incoherent, but nevertheless interesting interview given just prior to the start of the Stones' 1969 American tour. Mick discusses touring, the Beatles, his singing, his guitar playing, and other topics.

429. "Mick Jagger Talks to Lee Radziwill." By Lee Radziwill. *Interview.* Sept. 1972, pp. 7–9.

    Rather frivolous interview highlighted by some fine photos of Mick waterskiing and performing onstage.

430. "Mick Jagger — The Brain Behind The Rolling Stones." By Charles Peterson. *Pittsburgh Press.* Aug. 17, 1975, *Parade*, pp. 12, 15.

    Brief but perceptive look at Mick and the Stones, their history and current tour. Interesting primarily because of the source, a supplement which seldom features rock performers or counterculture viewpoints. Especially surprising are the photos of Jagger, including a cover which is a bit on the androgynous side.

431. "Mick Loves Bianca: The End of an Era." *Rock.* 2:3. June 21, 1971.

Wedding account by one of the leading rock newspapers. Humorously written report of what was to the *Rock* editors an almost incomprehensible event.

432. "Mr. Mick Jagger Speaks His Mind." By Stephen Jessel. *Times* (London). Aug. 1, 1967, p. 8a.

Interview with Mick recorded the day after he received a conditional discharge for his drug offense. Very enlightening, especially regarding British attitudes toward Mick, as expressed by their amazement at his civilized appearance and behavior. He discusses drugs, religion, politics, the generation gap, etc.

433. "Paint It Black, You Devil!" By Richard Neville. *Creem*. 3:26–30. Oct. 1971.

Slightly bitter appraisal of Mick by the beleaguered editor of *Oz*, who relates a stream of unkind, but somewhat humorous anecdotes. Neville questions Mick's political postures and lack of real commitment. This issue features a cover photo of Mick performing onstage.

434. "Random Notes." *Rolling Stone*. Nov. 26, 1970, p. 4.

Brief news note, interesting not so much for its account of the Rome concert, but rather for its description of Mick's beating up a photographer and being fined for it. Only account to date in which Mick physically assaults anyone.

435. "The Restless Generation." By Sheila More. *Times* (London). Dec. 11, 1968, p. 7a.

The *Times* attempts to understand various pop personalities, among them Mick, who expresses himself on parental relationships, marriage, money, etc.

436. "Table Talk with Mick in Paris." By Chris Hodenfield. *Rolling Stone.* Oct. 28, 1971, p. 10.

    Interview with Mick that was taped at l'Hotel in Paris while Mick was awaiting the birth of his daughter Jade. He reports on recent Stones decisions and future plans, including a tour of America.

437. "Talking About 'My Son, the Superstar'." By Boris Weintraub. *Washington Star-News.* July 26, 1974, p. 25.

    Conversation with Professor Joe Jagger about Mick in which he speaks freely and with considerable pride about his son both as a man and as a performing artist.

The Film *Ned Kelly*

438. "Australian Romp." By Charles E. Fager. *Christian Century.* 87:1386. Nov. 18, 1970.

    Humorous treatment of Jagger as Ned, in which his various inadequacies as a tough outlaw are discussed. Finally, Tony Richardson's direction is blasted.

*439. "Jagger as Outlaw." By A. H. Weiler. *New York Times.* Oct. 8, 1970, p. 62.

    Mixed review, in which Richardson receives some credit for his production, "*Ned Kelly* shimmers fitfully with varied beauties," and Jagger is regarded as at least adequate in the role of Ned. The film is one that, according to the reviewer, "bears all the signs of dedicated movie-making." Unfortunately, he concludes, it is a flawed work.

440. "Jagger's Acting Bow in Richardson's *Kelly*." By David Sterritt. *Christian Science Monitor.* June 22, 1970, p. 6.

Brief but interesting review in which both Jagger and Richardson are given *some* credit, the director for his "visual flair," the actor for his "pop-idol" presence, which the reviewer feels suits the part as long as "his famous mouth remains shut." Nevertheless, a more sympathetic review than some.

441. "Movie Chronicle." By William S. Pechter. *Commentary.* 50:90. Nov. 1970.

Unfavorable review, in which everyone is lambasted — Richardson for his artiness, Jagger for his role at Altamont.

*442. "*Ned Kelly*." By Margaret Tarratt. *Films and Filming.* 16:41–42. Aug. 1970.

Not too favorable review in which Richardson's direction is severely criticized. The reviewer suggests that Jagger's stage magnetism is lacking in this film and that he is "not quite big enough to dominate the film and carry it with him."

443. "*Ned Kelly*." *Screen World.* By John Willis. New York, Crown, 1971, pp. 160–161.

Two pages of photos from the film, no critical comments whatever.

The Film *Performance*

444. "A Completely Worthless Film." By Richard Schickel. *Life.* 69:6. Oct. 2, 1970.

   Typical of the shock and revulsion experienced by some reviewers, compounded by Schickel's special dislike for Jagger.

445. "Fine Performance, Shallow Film." By Michael Billington. *Illustrated London News.* 258:31. Jan. 16, 1971.

   Unfavorable, but rational and considered British review, in which James Fox is praised highly for his acting, but Mick Jagger is dismissed handily with the comment, "[he] said his lines and never bumped into the furniture." Includes photos from the film.

*446. "Jagger's *Performance* Devastating." By Leonard Brown. *Los Angeles Free Press.* Apr. 24, 1970, pp. 8–9.

   Written before the release of the film, this review in an underground paper is one of the most penetrating treatments of *Performance.* The review is highly favorable, giving great praise to both Cammell and Jagger. It also reports on the corporate changes at Warner Brothers that delayed the film and caused it to undergo extensive revision after completion. One of the few reviews to perceive what the film is all about.

*447. "A Last Word on *Performance.*" By Jack Kroll. *Art in America.* 59:114–115. Mar. 1971.

   Brilliant discourse on the film in an impeccable source, this is an extremely important retrospective review that explores the source of the film's theme in literature and life. The technical excellence of *Performance* is much admired. Sample quote: "The film's calculus of rhythms and images has that blazing virtuosity which is one of the primal pleasures in art." Includes photo of Jagger and Fox together.

448. "Mick's Duet." By Jay Cocks. *Time.* 96:61. Aug. 24, 1970.

Typical establishment reaction to the film; much horror, little comprehension, and a few inaccuracies in retelling of incidents. Also a review of *Ned Kelly* which is too slight to be cited.

*449. "The Most Loathsome Film of All." By John Simon. *New York Times.* Aug. 23, 1970, II, p. 1.

The third *Times* review, a bitter attack on the film, its makers, its star, and even its favorable reviewers. John Simon's dislike for Jagger is much in evidence and is given full rein. Though unbelievably harsh, the review is, without doubt, highly amusing and cleverly written.

*450. "One Emerges Feeling a Little Scorched, But . . ." By Peter Schjeldahl. *New York Times.* Aug. 16, 1970, II, p. 1.

The second *Times* review, highly favorable to all concerned, more serious than Greenspun's first review. Schjeldahl sees the film as highly important, is much impressed by Jagger, who, he says, "conveys a sense of personal liberty and spiritual knowingness that is thrilling." He concludes that the film is "something extraordinary."

*451. *"Performance."* By Philip French. *Sight and Sound.* 40: 67–69. Spring 1971.

An article, rather than just a review, it contains some of the most important statements to be made about the film. It is an in-depth discussion of the origins of Cammell's screenplay in the works of Jorge Luis Borges, as well as a thorough analysis of the cinematic techniques of co-directors Cammell and Roeg. The story is told in detail, and a number of stills from the film are included, among them a fine shot of Jagger as Turner that conveys his androgynous quality.

*452. *"Performance."* By Michael Goodwin. *Rolling Stone.* Sept. 3, 1970, p. 50.

This review, by the leading rock newspaper, is, appropriately, one of the few to emphasize the film's fine musical score. It also has high praise for the directors and, naturally, for its star, Mick Jagger, who the reviewer claims is "exquisite" in his role. His performance, according to Goodwin, "transcends acting to verge on psychodrama."

*453. *"Performance."* By Roger Greenspun. *New York Times.* Aug. 4, 1970, p. 21.

The first *Times* review saw the film in a fairly favorable light due to the presence of its two stars — Jagger and Fox — and also to its "sadism, masochism, decorative decadence, and languid omnisexuality." Greenspun's review caused a veritable barrage of criticism; various reviewers attacked him bitterly for his opinion. See, for example, John Simon in the *New York Times* (entry 449) and Richard Schickel in *Life* (entry 444).

454. "Under the Rock." By Paul D. Zimmerman. *Newsweek.* 76:85. Aug. 17, 1970.

This typically "straight" review is relieved by a few touches of humor and a final admission that Mick Jagger *does* have a "sexy presence" and "ability to deliver a line."

455. "Who's Right About *Performance?*" *New York Times.* Sept. 20, 1970, II, p. 12.

Various opinions are expressed in the "Movie Mailbag" column, most of which refer to John Simon's review.

Chronology

Author Index

Periodical Index

Chronology

1962

December 26   The Rolling Stones (not yet named) perform at the Picadilly Club. A disaster.

1963

February   They perform regularly as the house band at the Crawdaddy Club in Richmond, with increasing success.

April 29   Stones sign a contract with their new managers, Andrew Oldham and Eric Easton.

May 10   They record "Come On" in first official recording session.

June 7   First TV appearance in Britain on "Thank Your Lucky Stars." "Come On" is released.

June 30   "Come On" makes the Top 50 as number 50.

August 11   Appearance at National Jazz Festival in Richmond.

September 29   First English tour with Bo Diddley and the Everly Brothers.

November 1   "I Wanna Be Your Man"/"Stoned" released in Britain.

1964

January	*The Rolling Stones* (EP) released in Britain.
January 6	Tour of England with Ronettes.
February 21	"Not Fade Away" released in Britain.
April 26	Concert as Wembley Pool winners.
April 30	"Not Fade Away" a hit in America.
May 29	*The Rolling Stones* first LP in America.
June 1	First American tour, appearance on Dean Martin show soon after.
June 26	"It's All Over Now" released.
June 27	Controversial appearance on "Juke Box Jury."
August	*5 X 5* (EP) released in Britain.
August 8	Concert at The Hague, Jagger's first news item in the *Times,* an arrest for speeding and driving without a license.
September 5	English tour with Chuck Berry, the Mojos, Charlie and Inez Fox.
September 10	Named "Most Popular British Group" by *Melody Maker,* "Not Fade Away" named best song.
October	The album *12 X 5* released in America.
October 20	First Paris show at the Olympia.
October 26	Second American tour begins.
November 13	"Little Red Rooster" released, Stones refused right to perform in South Africa by Musician's Union.

December 21	Charlie Watts's book on Charlie Parker is published, entitled *Ode to a High Flying Bird*.

1965

January 6–8	Tour of Ireland.
January 21	Tour of Australia and New Zealand begins.
February	*Rolling Stones Now!* released in America.
February 16–17	Concerts in Singapore and Hong Kong.
February 26	"Last Time"/"Play with Fire" released. "Time Is on My Side" released in United Kingdom.
March 5	English tour with Chuck Berry and the Hollies, followed by Scandinavian tour.
April 17–18	Concerts at the Olympia, Paris.
April 22	Third American tour begins.
May 13	"(I Can't Get No) Satisfaction" released.
June 15–18	Tour of Scotland.
June 24–29	Tour of Scandinavia.
July	*Out of Our Heads* released in America.
July 23	Stones fined for "public insult." (Having been refused permission to use the men's room, the Stones urinated on the wall of a garage.)
August 1	London Palladium appearance in which they refused to go on the revolving stage for the finale, the first group ever to flout this tradition.
September 3–5	Tour of Ireland, "Satisfaction" top hit in America.

October	"Get Off My Cloud" is released, fourth American tour begins.
November	The album *December's Children* released.

1966

January 1	New Year's Eve appearance on "Ready, Steady, Go."
February 4	"19th Nervous Breakdown" released.
February 13	Appearance on Ed Sullivan show.
February 18–March 1	Australian tour.
March 26–April 5	European tour.
March	The album *Big Hits (High Tide and Green Grass)* released.
April	"Paint It Black" released.
May 11	The Stones consider filming *Only Lovers Left Alive,* then decide against it.
June	The album *Aftermath* is released in America.
June 24	Fifth American tour begins. The Stones rent the yacht *Sea Panther* to live on while in New York, having been refused reservations by fourteen New York hotels.
September	"Have You Seen Your Mother, Baby?" released.
September 23	British tour begins with Yardbirds, Ike and Tina Turner at the Royal Albert Hall.

November   The live album *Got Live If You Want It!* released.

December 10   *New Musical Express* names Stones "Best Rhythm & Blues Group in Britain." Best song: "Satisfaction."

1967

January   The album *Between the Buttons* is released.

January 13   Stones appear on Ed Sullivan show, "Let's Spend the Night Together" released in America.

February 7   Jagger files libel suit against *News of the World*.

February 12   Police raid Keith Richard's house, seeking drugs.

March 18   Jagger and Richard are served with summons on drug charges.

March 25–
April 17   European tour.

May 10   Jagger and Richard appear in court on drug charges and are released on bail. Brian Jones is arrested in his London home and charged with unlawful possession of drugs.

June   The album *Flowers* is released.

June 27   Jagger and Richard are found guilty on drug charges.

June 29   Jagger is jailed at Brixton, Richard at Wormwood Scrubs.

June 30	They are granted bail on appeal and released from prison.
July 1	The *Times* editorial appears: "Who Breaks a Butterfly on a Wheel?" It is an eloquent defense of the two Stones' right to be treated as ordinary citizens in the courts.
July 31	The appeals court lifts sentences of Jagger and Richard. Jagger is given a "conditional discharge," Richard is freed.
August 18	"We Love You" is released.
September 15	Jagger is detained in New York by immigration officials as a drug offender.
October 30	Brian Jones sentenced to prison for possession of cannabis.
October 31	Brian is released from prison on appeal.
November	The album *Their Satanic Majesties Request* is released.
December 12	The appeals court sets aside Brian's sentence.
December 15	Brian is hospitalized.

1968

March 18	Serafina Watts is born to Charlie and Shirley.
May 12	First Stones public concert in Britain in two years takes place at *New Musical Express* Pollwinners' Concert. (Brian's last public performance with the Stones.)

May 21	Brian is again arrested for possession of cannabis, is released on bail.
May 25	"Jumpin' Jack Flash" is released.
June 11	Brian again on trial on drug charges.
July 26	Cover controversy prevents scheduled release of *Beggars Banquet*.
August	"Street Fighting Man" is released.
September 4	"Street Fighting Man" is banned from air play in America.
September 26	Brian is fined for possession of cannabis.
November	*Beggars Banquet* is released in America. The cover is a compromise with London Records who refuse to distribute the Stones' "graffiti" selection.
December 12	"Rock and Roll Circus" TV show is videotaped.

1969

January 13	Brian loses appeal and his drug conviction is upheld.
May 28	Mick and Marianne Faithfull arrested for possession of cannabis.
June 9	Brian quits Stones following clash with other group members.
June 13	Mick Taylor joins group as Brian's replacement.
June 30	"Honky Tonk Women" and "You Can't Always Get What You Want" released in America.

July 3	Brian Jones is found dead in his swimming pool.
July 5	Hyde Park concert is played as a memorial to Brian.
July 6	Jagger leaves for Australia with Marianne to star in *Ned Kelly*.
July 8	Marianne is hospitalized in Australia for a drug overdose.
July 10	The funeral of Brian Jones.
August	"Through the Past, Darkly" is released in America.
August 10	Keith Richard's son Marlon is born to Anita Pallenberg.
August 18	Jagger is accidentally shot in the hand while filming *Ned Kelly*.
September 12	Mick and Marianne return to England.
October 17	Stones arrive in Los Angeles for start of American tour.
November	The album *Let It Bleed* released in America.
November 7	Start of sixth American tour at Fort Collins, Colorado.
November 27–28	Climax of tour at Madison Square Garden.
November 30	End of tour at West Palm Beach Pop Festival.
December 1	Stones record at Muscle Shoals, Alabama, for forthcoming album.

December 6	Free concert at Altamont, California.
December 12	Stones play at Saville Theatre, London.
December 19	Jagger appears in court on charges of possessing cannabis, is found guilty as charged. Marianne Faithfull is acquitted.
December 21	Stones play Christmas concert at Lyceum Ballroom in London.

1970

January 27	Jagger is fined for possession of cannabis, charges arresting officer with attempted bribery.
March 11	The film *Sympathy for the Devil* opens in New York.
April 8	Inquiry into bribery allegation by Jagger.
May 5	Detective is cleared of bribery allegation.
July 30	Stones announce plan to negotiate a new record contract.
August 3	*Performance* starring Jagger opens in New York.
September 2– October 9	First European tour since 1967.
September 8	*Get Yer Ya Ya's Out!* released, live album of 1969 U. S. tour.
October 7	*Ned Kelly* starring Jagger opens in New York.
November 26	Jagger visits Ahmet Ertegun in Nassau to discuss distribution rights contract for new record

label. He is accompanied by his future wife, Bianca de Macias.

December 6   *Gimme Shelter* opens in New York on the anniversary of the Altamont free concert.

1971

March 4–14   Stones' Farewell to Britain tour, after which they depart for new residences in France.

April 1   The Stones' new label announced by its new head, Marshall Chess, son of Chess Records' founder.

April 6   New record contract is signed with Kinney/Atlantic. Stones label will be run by their international corporation based in Geneva, with branches in New York and London.

April 13   The single "Brown Sugar" is released by Rolling Stones Records.

April 30   The album *Sticky Fingers* is released.

May 12   Mick Jagger is married to Bianca de Macias in St. Tropez, France.

July 23   Stones sue former manager Allen Klein for $7.5 million, charging mismanagement of funds.

July 29   *Gimme Shelter* opens in London at the Rialto.

August 19   Stones sue former managers Andrew Oldham and Eric Easton charging mismanagement of funds.

October 21   Mick Jagger's daughter Jade is born to his wife Bianca in Paris.

November | An American tour is announced for spring '72 at which time a new album will be released. Stones take up residence in Los Angeles to prepare for tour.

1972

January | The album *Hot Rocks: 1964–1971* is released by London Records.

January 8 | Jagger is selected for the 1971 International Best Dressed List.

April | Jagger vacations with wife Bianca and daughter Jade on the island of Bora Bora.

May 22 | The album *Exile on Main Street* is released.

June 3 | Stones begin their North American tour at Vancouver's Pacific Coliseum. The opening is marred by violence.

July 4 | Stones put on Fourth of July show at Kennedy Stadium in Washington, D. C.

July 17 | An equipment truck is damaged by a bomb in Montreal.

July 18 | Stones arrested in Warwick, Rhode Island, airport for alleged assault on a news photographer and police.

July 19 | They perform after midnight at the Boston Garden, four hours late, after release from jail and a trip to Boston under police motorcycle escort.

July 24 | Stones open at Madison Square Garden.

July 25	Stones perform matinee and evening shows at the Garden.
July 26	Mick Jagger's birthday is celebrated at the Garden during final concert in New York at end of tour. Mick's party continues at the St. Regis afterward.
August	Mick and Bianca vacation at a friend's house in Montauk, Long Island.
December	The album *More Hot Rocks* is released by London Records.
December 5	Warrants are issued in France for the arrest of Keith Richard and Anita Pallenberg on drug charges.
December 27	Mick and Bianca fly to Nicaragua to search for her mother, missing in earthquake. She is found unharmed.

1973

January 2	The Rolling Stones are named top group album artists of 1972 according to *Billboard, Cash Box,* and *Record World.*
January 3	Mick and Bianca are named to the 1972 International Best Dressed List.
January 9	Japanese officials refuse entry to Japan to Mick Jagger because of marijuana conviction in England. The tour of Japan is cancelled.
January 18	Stones perform benefit concert at Inglewood Forum in Los Angeles for Nicaraguan earthquake victims.

January 21–22   Hawaii concerts.

February   Jagger is named top vocalist and voted into Hall of Fame in *Playboy* Jazz/Pop Poll. Stones are voted tops in vocal groups.

February 5–27   Hong Kong, New Zealand, and Australian tour.

June 19   Marsha Hunt claims in court that Mick Jagger is the father of her two-year-old daughter Karis. Jagger denies the charge and flies to Rome on business.

June 26   Police raid the home of Keith Richard and arrest him on charges of possessing unlawful guns and marijuana.

September   The album *Goats Head Soup* is released.

September 1   European tour begins in Vienna.

September 9   The Stones perform at Wembley Pool in London, the highlight of their tour of Britain. They celebrate London appearance by renting Blenheim Palace for a grand party.

October 19   European tour ends in West Berlin.

December   Keith Richard is fined $500 for possession of drugs and unregistered weapons.

1974

April 16   The film *Ladies and Gentlemen, the Rolling Stones* opens at the Ziegfeld Theater in New York. The planned street fair is cancelled by city authorities.

May	Bill Wyman's solo album *Monkey Grip* is released.
July	Mick Jagger's younger brother Chris performs at the Bottom Line in New York, the beginning of a series of club dates featuring the singer/writer.
July 26	Mick and Bianca celebrate his birthday with a garden party in London. Mick attends in cropped hair and a "Fred Astaire" suit, according to *Women's Wear Daily*.
July 28	Tony Scaduto is interviewed about his biography of Jagger. "I wrote it almost as a novel without distorting the facts," he stated. He then concluded, "I dig the Stones' music. I just don't like Mick Jagger. I think he's a creep."
July 30	Mick Jagger's father, Professor Joe Jagger, is interviewed about his famous son. Among other favorable comments about Mick, Professor Jagger states, "Mick could have been a marvelous cricketeer."
October	The album *It's Only Rock 'n' Roll* is released.

1975

March 17	The Stones are denied entrance into the Soviet Union because "they lack glamour, attractiveness, naturalness and novelty" and would not "help people to achieve self-perfection."
May 1	The Stones give a ten-minute performance from a flatbed truck outside of Fifth Avenue Hotel in

New York, by way of announcing their forth-coming Tour of the Americas.

May 17   Mick Jagger is injured when he thrusts his hand through a glass door .pane in a restaurant in Montauk. He receives twenty stitches at South-ampton Hospital but expects no delay in the Stones' American tour.

June 1   The band performs the first concert of its Tour of the Americas as scheduled in Baton Rouge, Louisiana.

June 1   The album *Metamorphosis* is released by ABKCO. The album *Made in the Shade* is re-leased by Rolling Stone Records.

June 3   San Antonio authorities force the Stones to eliminate the inflatable phallus from their show on the grounds that it is obscene.

June 5   The Stones visit the Alamo and Jagger poses for photographers draped in a Union Jack.

June 22   Opening night in New York.

July 5   Keith Richard is arrested in Fordyce, Arkansas, and charged with reckless driving and posses-sion of an illegal knife. Richard was released the same day.

July 9   Opening night in Los Angeles.

August 4 Concert at Louisville (Freedom Hall) is added to itinerary.

August 6 Concert at Hampton Roads (Coliseum) is added to itinerary.

August 8	"Farewell Concert" at Buffalo's Rich Stadium ends 1975 tour.
August 19	Jagger testifies in Oakland, California, that he is not responsible for damages to ranchers' property during the Altamont concert.
August 25	Oakland, California, court rules Jagger innocent on charges of assaulting a process server.
December 14	Chilean government refuses Stones permission to give concert on Easter Island on the basis that the island would be irreparably damaged.

1976

April	The album *Black and Blue* is released.
April 28	Opening concert of European tour in Frankfurt.
May 19	Keith Richard is arrested on suspicion of possession of drugs after unidentified substance is found in his car.
May 21	Concert at Earl's Court, London.
June 14	Fracas develops between Stones' bodyguards and French Hell's Angels on Riviera. Eleven persons are injured.
June 23	Last concert of European tour in Vienna.
August 22	Concert at Knebworth Fair; 200,000 fans attend what is billed as possibly final performance by band.

1977

March 2   Keith Richard is arrested in Toronto on charges of trafficking in heroin.

March 4–5   Stones perform at El Mocambo nightclub in Toronto to invited audience. Show is recorded for inclusion on forthcoming live album. Margaret Trudeau attends both shows.

March 10   Margaret Trudeau denies romance with either Mick Jagger or Ron Wood. Mick Jagger denies romance with Margaret Trudeau.

March 15   Anita Pallenberg pleads guilty to possession of marijuana and hashish and is fined $400.

April 1   Warwick, Rhode Island, court ends action to try Richard and Jagger for respectively assaulting a news photographer and obstructing a police officer during 1975 American tour.

October   The album *Love You Live* is released. Performances from the 1976 European tour and the El Mocambo shows are included.

December 2   Keith loses motion to have heroin traffic charge reduced to simple possession at Toronto court hearing.

December 6   Keith elects trial by judge and jury on two drug charges at preliminary hearing in Toronto.

Author Index

Periodical Index